"Surviving was my inheritance; thriving became my choice. Turns out, you don't need a fairy godparent, just a sense of humor and the courage to heal."

WHO NEEDS SANTA

& OTHER LESSONS IN SURVIVING TOXIC PARENTS

S.Y. VIDAL

Published by Rosemary Woodlands Publishing
San Juan, Puerto Rico USA
www.rosemarywoodlands.com
First Edition
ISBN: 979-8-9911231-0-5
Printed in the United States of America

*This book is a work of non-fiction. Names, characters,
places, and incidents are the product of the author's
experience. Any resemblance to actual persons, living or
dead, or actual events is intentional.*

For anyone else who needs a light at the end of the tunnel.

"Life didn't promise to be wonderful, but that doesn't mean it can't be. Your story begins where their influence ends."

— S.Y. Vidal

CONTENTS

CHAPTER 1

AN INTRODUCTION: PREPARING TO UNPACK THE BAGGAGE

Here's the thing about growing up with toxic parents: it's a lot like trying to play an intense game of dodgeball but blindfolded. Oh, and on a battlefield full of landmines. Sound a little dramatic? Yeah, that's the funny thing about humor—it's often a shield, a way to soften the blows of a reality that's otherwise too painful to bear.

You can call me Scotty, and this book is my story. It's a tale of resilience, survival, and, eventually finding humor in the darkest corners. You might laugh, you might cry, shit, you might even cringe a little; but by the end, you'll realize that no matter what hand you've been dealt, you have the power to shuffle the deck.

I didn't grow up with the typical nuclear family. Instead, I was born into a world of neglect and abuse under the watchful eye of a narcissistic mother. She was the architect of my childhood, a puppet master pulling the strings of a life filled with chaos, lies, and pain. As a kid, even as an adult, I was never really living—I was surviving. But here's the thing about survival mode: while it may keep you going, it doesn't let you grow. It wasn't until my twenties, after a wake-up call that landed me behind bars, that I realized something had to change.

That's when I began a journey of self-discovery, healing, and transformation. I had to learn how to untangle the knots of my past, construct a life rooted in love rather than fear, and ultimately, laugh in the face of adversity.

This is a book about breaking free from the chains of toxic parenthood, but it's so much more than just my story. It's a story that's been lived by far too many people, and it's a story that needs to be told. So, if you're reading this, know you're not alone. Whether you're struggling with the echoes of your tumultuous past or simply curious about navigating life's many curveballs, I welcome you to this journey.

Let's set the stage. I'm a millennial - one of those avocado toast-loving, student debt-laden Individuals with whom the media has a field day. I'm also a queer man with a sense of humor that's as dark as a fresh pot of coffee. You know, the kind you chug down at 2 a.m. when binge-watching that show that was only cool to talk about six months ago. But I digress. This book is about something much heavier than streaming series or hipster breakfasts. It's about the crushing weight of parental neglect and abuse and how it can shape us in ways we never signed up for. It's about dealing with the fallout from a generation that, bless their hearts, couldn't quite grasp the whole "nurturing" part of parenting. But don't worry, we're not here to sit in a circle and sob about our unfortunate upbringings. No, we're here to recognize our past, confront it head-on, and learn how to heal. And we'll laugh too - because laughter, my friends, can be the best damn medicine.

So why am I, your Britney-loving guide, qualified to embark on this journey with you? My childhood was a bit like a rollercoaster ride. A haunted rollercoaster. You know, the kind where the safety bar doesn't quite click down all the way, and you spend the entire time clutching the seat, wondering if you're about to be catapulted into the abyss. But I made it through that wild ride, and now I want to help you navigate yours.

In this book, we'll be digging deep into the sticky tar pits of the past. We'll explore the different forms of parental neglect and abuse - the physical, the emotional, and the verbal. We'll talk about how survival mode can kick in and leave you treading water for far longer than you'd like.

But don't worry. We'll also talk about the climb out of that pit and the fantastic view once you're standing on solid ground again. Because here's the thing: the climb isn't just a dull, grey trudge uphill. Sure, it can be a struggle - you may stumble, get dirty, and sometimes find yourself crying in a diner at 3 a.m., but on that climb, you're also growing stronger with each step. With every rock you stumble over, you're proving to yourself and the world that you're more than your past.

And the view? *Let me paint you a picture.* It's not just the satisfaction of looking back and seeing how far you've come - though that's a heady rush of triumph all on its own. No, it's more than that. It's the feeling of standing tall on firm ground, knowing that you scaled that mountain yourself. It's the sight of a future stretching out before you, a future you shape on your terms.

Through this journey, you will rediscover yourself, not as a victim or a survivor, but as a fighter and a conqueror. You'll learn that you are stronger than you've ever imagined and that your capacity for healing is immense. The best part? You won't be alone. We're in this together, navigating through the rocky slopes of past trauma toward the pinnacle of healing.

And yes, we will definitely laugh along the way. Humor will be our trusty pickaxe - helping us chip away at the mountain, lightening our load, and occasionally being the only thing keeping us sane. Because let's be real, if we can't laugh at the absurdity of life sometimes, we'd all be weeping into our iced coffees.

You might be sitting with various emotions. That's normal. This isn't an easy journey, and it's not meant to be breezed through. But trust me, you've got this. After all, you're a rock climber now, and every rock climber knows the importance of a good plan. Before diving into the deep end, let's pause momentarily and lay out our **Action Plan**. This is an *'Emotional Toolkit'* that'll help us navigate the rough terrain ahead. Just as a climber would only venture up a mountain with the right gear, we will ensure we're adequately prepared for this journey.

Here's what we're going to do:

1. Self-Awareness Check

Our first step on this journey is akin to peering into a mirror, but instead of checking out our physical reflection, we're taking a good, hard look at our emotional selves.

As we stand on the precipice of unearthing the impacts of our past, it's time to take stock of our current emotional state. It's time to peel back the layers of our emotions and delve deep into our feelings about our upbringing and relationships with our parents.

This might sound daunting, and believe me, it can be, but it's also an invaluable step in our healing journey because acknowledging where we are is the first step to determining where we want to go. While it can be uncomfortable to face these feelings, it's necessary.

So, how do we go about this?

You might find solitude conducive for reflection. Take some time alone in a comfortable and quiet place. Consider your past, your relationship with your parents, and how these elements have impacted your life. Remember, there's no right or wrong way to feel. Your feelings are your own, and they're valid, no matter what they are. Alternatively, it is helpful to journal about your feelings. Writing can be a powerful tool for exploration and discovery. You could start by answering prompts like "*How* does thinking about my childhood make me feel?" or "When I think about my relationship with my parents, I feel..." And as you write, allow yourself to be honest and raw. This journal is for you and you alone.

The process of self-awareness is a vulnerable one. It might even be uncomfortable. But remember, this is the first step toward healing, toward understanding ourselves better. It's like tuning your guitar before a performance or calibrating your compass before a hike. It sets the stage for what's to come.

Remember, we're doing this to unburden ourselves and shed the weight of the past we've been carrying for far too long. This isn't about laying blame or dwelling on the past but understanding and acknowledging our feelings. It's about giving our history a nod, recognizing its impact, and then using that understanding as a stepping stone toward healing.

2.   Establish a Safe Space

Every journey is easier when you have a safe harbor, a place to retreat when the going gets tough. As we start to unpack some of the painful experiences from your past, it's incredibly important that you have such a space. Think of this safe space as your own personal sanctuary. It should be a place that brings you comfort, calm, and a sense of security. For some, this might be a cozy nook in your home. It could be your bedroom, where you can curl up with a blanket, surrounded by your favorite books and trinkets. Or it's your living room, where you can sit with a comforting cup of tea, basking in the warm glow of your favorite scented candle. Nature might be the key to creating that feeling of safety for others. You could find your haven in a tranquil corner of your local park, where you can sit quietly and be soothed by leaves rustling in the wind and birds chirping in the trees. Your safe space could even be less physical and more about time. Perhaps it's that quiet period in the early morning when the world is still mostly asleep, and you can feel like you have a moment just for yourself. Or it's late at night when the world has quieted down, and you can ponder the stars.

The point is that your safe space should be uniquely yours. It should be a place (or time) where you can take a deep breath and feel a sense of peace. It's OK to prioritize your comfort and mental well-being. In fact, it's essential. This journey into your past isn't about punishing yourself. It's about understanding, healing, and ultimately, growing. Your safe space is your aid station on this path - a place where you can rest, recharge, and remind yourself that you're taking these steps for your well-being. Spend a little time thinking about what your ideal safe space looks like. Cultivate, cherish, and remember it's always there for you when you need a respite.

3. Be Ready to Laugh

Let's talk about laughter. It may seem odd, even a little inappropriate, to emphasize humor when we're about to delve into some heavy topics but hear me out. Laughter is a bit like an emotional Swiss Army knife. It's versatile, useful in countless situations, and often differentiates between coping and crumbling. Science backs this up. Laughter can reduce stress, improve mood, and even boost your immune system. Perhaps most importantly, it can create a sense of distance, a breathing space between you and your pain. It has the unique ability to bring light to the darkest corners, help us see our struggles from a fresh perspective, and remind us that joy can be found even during pain.

As we dive into the deep end, remember that it's OK to laugh. In fact, it's more than OK - it's a form of self-care. It's saying, "Yes, I've been through hell, but I can still find humor in the world." It's a form of resilience and resistance, affirming our ability to rise above our pain.

To prepare for this, think about what makes you laugh. What kind of humor resonates with you? Slapstick comedy? Witty puns? Absurd memes? Quirky cartoon shows? An excellent stand-up special on Netflix? Gather these things and keep them handy. Bookmark that hilarious YouTube video. Write down that joke that always makes you chuckle. Re-watch that episode of your favorite sitcom that always leaves you in stitches. It was always *The Nanny* for me!

These aren't just distractions. They're part of your toolkit. They remind us that no matter how deep we delve into our past, we can always resurface for fresh, laughter-filled air. So go ahead, laugh it up. Your journey through healing isn't just about confronting pain; it's about reclaiming joy. And laughter, dear reader, is a vital part of that joy.

4. Set Your Intentions

This step is all about setting your personal compass. You've picked up this book, which is a significant first step. Now, it's time to reflect on why you're embarking on this journey.

What are you hoping to achieve? Are you seeking understanding? Are you looking to unpack and unravel the tangled web of your past to gain a clearer insight into how your upbringing has shaped the person you are today? Or maybe you're seeking to heal, looking to mend the wounds that might still be raw, to find a way to move beyond the hurt and the pain?

It could be a combination of understanding and healing you're after. The two often go hand in hand. By understanding our past, we can better comprehend our present and find the path to recovery.

Take a few moments to really delve into your motivations. It's not about setting concrete goals like you might do at a fitness class. No 'Lose 10 pounds of emotional baggage in 10 days' type promises here. This journey is far too personal and complex for that. Your intentions can be as simple as wanting to wake up one day without feeling the weight of your past or as profound as striving to break a generational cycle of abuse.

It's OK for your intentions to change as you progress through this book. You might begin this journey seeking understanding, and as you gain clarity, you might realize that what you truly want is to heal. Or you might start with the goal of healing and then recognize that you first need to understand to truly heal. The critical thing is to stay in tune with yourself, to listen to your inner voice as we navigate through the chapters to come. Your intentions will serve as your guiding light, illuminating your path as we traverse the rocky terrain of past trauma. So take some time, set your compass, and prepare for the journey ahead. You're stronger than you know, and I'll be here with you every step of the way.

5. Find a Support System

No matter how self-reliant we are, humans are, by nature, social creatures. We thrive on connection and support from others, especially during personal growth and change. While confronting your past and healing is a deeply personal journey, having a support system can make the process smoother and more manageable.

Think of your support system as your personal cheerleading squad - the people who cheer you on during the highs, support you through the lows and provide a listening ear or a comforting hug when needed. This could be a trusted friend who has shown understanding and empathy in the past or a family member who has always been there for you. If you're comfortable doing so, consider sharing your intentions for this journey with them. Let them know that you're about to embark on a healing path, and their support would mean the world to you.

For some, a professional like a therapist can be an invaluable part of this support system. Therapists are trained to help you navigate complex emotions and guide you through painful experiences. If you're already seeing a therapist, great! If not, consider finding one. It's perfectly OK to shop around until you find a therapist you click with. I did! Trust me, the right therapist is like a sturdy rope for a rock climber - they won't pull you up the mountain, but they'll be there to catch you if you stumble.

In addition to individual support, consider joining a support group. Being part of a group can be incredibly empowering. It's a safe space to share your experiences, fears, and triumphs with people who have faced similar issues. Remember, there's strength in numbers. A group can provide a sense of community and belonging, reassuring you that you're not alone in your journey.

Creating a support system might take time, and that's OK. Don't rush it. Like choosing the right climbing gear, selecting the people and resources that feel right for you is essential. Remember, your support system is there for your benefit - to encourage, support, and celebrate you as you make this incredible journey. So choose wisely, and don't hesitate to reach out when needed. After all, even the best rock climbers need a little support sometimes.

Remember, this journey is yours; you can navigate it at your own pace. You are not alone, and it's OK to ask for help when you need it.

CHAPTER 2

THROUGH THE LOOKING GLASS: MY ROLLER-COASTER CHILDHOOD

Welcome to the untidy shop of horrors and delights, I call my childhood. If my past was a place, it would be a thrift store filled with everything from glorious, gleaming trinkets of joy to old, moth-eaten scraps of sadness. I'm inviting you in, but don't say I didn't warn you—it's a mess here!

Imagine walking into this peculiar little store. Every shelf is a jumble of objects, each a memento from my rollercoaster of a life. Some things might make you laugh, others... well, they might make you want to leave the store immediately, and that's perfectly fine. I've been trying to get out for years!

Now, this isn't any old antique store; oh no, this is the bizarre bazaar of my existence, each item a piece of a puzzle, whispering tales of laughter and tears. And overseeing it all, like a shadow lurking in every corner, is the formidable presence of my mother—a character so vibrant, so overwhelming, you'd think she walked out of a Shakespearean tragedy, minus the eloquence and with double the drama.

This isn't going to be a walk down memory lane; it's more of a stumbling run through a bramble bush of the past, where each thorn is a memory, each scratch a scar of the soul. I'm your guide on this wacky adventure, helping you navigate through the chaos and clutter of my life, pointing out the landmines, and occasionally tripping on them myself.

Remember, in this haphazard collection, you'll find not only fragments of pain but also shards of resilience, bits of a spirit that refused to be broken, that learned to laugh in the face of adversity. Yes, I learned to find humor even in the darkest places, and believe me, with my mother, it was either laugh or cry, and I mainly chose to laugh.

Strap in and let's dive headfirst into this whirlwind journey through a labyrinth of light and shadows, unraveling the tangled threads of my existence, discovering the melody in the racket, the sweet in the bitter, the sanity in the madness. It will be a wild, crazy, heartbreaking, and hilarious ride through the cluttered aisles of my life and the convoluted corridors of my past.

To truly grasp the essence of my journey, it's pivotal to understand the storm that was my mother. She was not the beacon of warmth and nurture that mothers are often pictured as. My mother was quite the character, one filled with contradictions and shadows. Think less Carol Brady and more Cersei Lannister, without any instinct to protect her young.

She existed in a world of her own, a realm filled with the echoes of her trauma, drowned out by the noise of her pursuit of attention and transient joys. Motherhood seemed a distant, blurry concept to her, lost amid her turbulent quests for validation and desire. Her days weren't about nurturing or protecting but about chasing after fleeting shadows and running from her own ghosts.

Her existence was like a series of disjointed scenes from a drama, every moment a play for attention, every action a rebellion against unseen chains. Bottles and men were her constant companions, each drowning out the whispers of responsibility and duty. The role of a nurturing, caring mother wasn't in her script; she was the lead actress in her own tragic play, where the cries of her children were just background noise to her soliloquies of suffering.

To paint the picture clearly, she was more intrigued by the reflections in her glass of beer than by the eyes of her children looking up to her. Her days and nights blended into a canvas painted with the hues of neglect and abandonment, a masterpiece of her own making, a gallery displaying her eternal struggle with her demons.

My mother was a lot of things. She was sometimes a tempest, tossing everything around her into a whirlwind of chaos. At others, she'd become strangely introspective, as if she was having a silent, internal tug-of-war. Every so often, she'd unload stories of her younger days between the volcanic outbursts and the ensuing cold wars. These weren't the usual nostalgic, sepia-toned tales one might expect from a parent. No, her narrative was akin to a tattered diary full of scribbles, with ink blots marring the pages. Each tale is more tragic, more somber. A heartbreak here, a betrayal there, and an overarching theme of navigating life amidst a perennial storm.

But you know what was the most jarring part? The way she spoke of her love for her children, for me. It was as if she believed that by merely saying these words, she could right every wrong and mend every scar. She had this peculiar habit of juxtaposing her vocal love anthems with her chaotic concerto of actions. It was like trying to jam out to a rock ballad immediately followed by a jarring jazz improvisation. Nothing synced.

Have you ever tried to solve a jigsaw puzzle with pieces from different sets? That was my mom in a nutshell. Each piece is a fragment of her traumatic past, none fitting snugly with the other. It wasn't just her story either. Grandma was her own brand of Pandora's Box. The tales of her escapades, battles, and heartaches painted a clear picture – this was a generational gig. Like a family heirloom, pain and trauma were handed down, adorned with new embellishments by each generation.

In my quest for understanding, I sometimes wondered if, in her skewed way, she thought her actions were a bizarre display of love. Maybe in the rollercoaster of her psyche, the sharp drops and harrowing loops were her way of preparing us for the world. Yet, recognizing this carousel of generational chaos doesn't make the ride any smoother. It only gives me a map of the tracks. While it doesn't provide justification, it does offer a window into her world, helping pave a path toward some semblance of understanding. After all, every storm has an eye, a center of calm. And in sifting through the tales of her past, I can find that elusive calm amidst the chaos.

In this chaotic symphony, I, a young, queer, hopeful kid, had dreams and aspirations that seemed like far-fetched fantasies. The simple joy of owning a Barbie seemed like a distant star, and learning to wade through the turbulent waters of my mother's whims and fancies was like learning to dance to the tunes of a broken record.

Every day was a battle, a navigation through the storm of her erratic moods, a journey through the shadows cast by her unhealed wounds. It was a constant tug-of-war between hope and despair, a dance between longing for a loving embrace and facing the stark reality of her cold, indifferent world.

As we take those tentative steps into the oddities of my past, the first item we stumble upon is a dusty animated Santa figurine. Doesn't he look cheerful with his red cheeks and belly that shakes like a bowl full of jelly? Well, don't let that fool you; this little guy is a seasoned veteran of emotional warfare, a silent observer of a night when my mother played the Grinch who stole not just Christmas but my childhood innocence.

Now, lean in close, and you can almost hear the clash of battle, the wails of a disillusioned child, the cruel, cutting words of a mother more monster than Santa's helper. This figurine is a mute relic of a confrontation that replaced visions of sugar plums with the stinging slap of reality.

"*Did you go into my room?*" My mother's voice was a serrated edge, every syllable meant to cut, to wound. Her eyes, ablaze with a mix of fury and something darker, bore into mine, searching, accusing.

"*No, Mom, I swear I didn't! I was drawing,*" my voice was a whisper, a feeble attempt to push back against the towering tsunami of her rage.

"*Liar!*" Her hand connected with my cheek, the sting immediate, the heat radiating from the point of impact. "*You ruin everything! Everything is always about you!*"

I could feel the warmth of tears, a mix of pain and fear, but I dared not let them fall. "*Mom, please, I didn't go into your room. I didn't see the gifts!*"

"*You wanted to ruin Santa for yourself, didn't you?*" She spat, her face inches from mine, her breath hot against my skin.

"*I didn't! I promise I didn't!*" The dam broke, tears flowing freely now, sobs choking my words.

"*You've spoiled Christmas for yourself!*" she roared, each word a nail in the coffin of my childhood beliefs, each slap a blow to my confidence.

Her onslaught was relentless, every word a new wound, every accusation a fresh scar. I was trapped, cornered by her unyielding anger, her uncompromising rage. I was just a child, lost, confused, and broken, a pawn in her twisted game, a casualty in her war against herself. The weight of her words, accusations, and anger was crushing and suffocating. And so, to stop the pain, to end the torment, I confessed to a crime I didn't commit, admitted to a sin I didn't conceive. It was a desperate bid for mercy and a respite from her relentless assault. It was surrender, a white flag raised in the face of overwhelming force.

In the wake of her victory, I was left to pick up the pieces of my shattered beliefs to rebuild a world where the magic of Christmas was just a cruel joke, a bitter lie. The joy of the season was tainted, the sparkle of the lights dimmed, the laughter of the elves silenced. I was no longer a child, my innocence lost, my dreams crushed under her wrath.

In reality on that wintery afternoon, amidst the anticipation of Christmas, Mom bustled in from her latest shopping adventure. Little bro, ever her shadow, trailed behind, his tiny steps mirroring her hurried ones. Their voices, a cocktail of festive excitement and weariness, faded as she disappeared into her room, depositing her new purchases. I sat in our trailer's dining room, engrossed, my pencil dancing on paper, capturing the iconic visages of The Simpsons, inspired by some kitschy artwork on a fast-food cup. But as ever, in the periphery of my focus was the world around me, the quirks and dramas of our familial universe.

Suddenly, out toddled my brother, glee evident in his eyes as he waved about a Fischer Price remote control police car—a probable Christmas surprise mistakenly unveiled. However, in Mom's world, where narratives often deviated from reality, I was painted as the villain. To her, I was the one who'd intruded into her sanctuary, pilfering presents. That confrontation, that night of lost innocence, was a defining moment in my life, a turning point in my journey. It's the starting point of a path marked with shadows, paved with pain, and steeped in sorrow. It's the prologue to a story of resilience, survival, finding the strength to rise above the darkness, seeing the light in the shadows, and dancing in the rain.

That night was just one of the many episodes where I felt unloved and unseen. The consistency of such confrontations left me clinging to fleeting moments of happiness, like singing songs like "The Oak Tree" with her during joyrides in her EXP, a bright spot amidst the gloom. They were brief, but in those moments, the chaos faded, replaced by a sense of normalcy, a glimpse into what could have been. For every positive memory, ten more served as painful reminders of the chasm between us. Still, they taught me an invaluable lesson—life isn't about waiting for the skies to clear but finding beauty amid the clouds. And find it, I did, using the pain, the anger, and the sadness as stepping stones, transforming them into resilience, empathy, and an unyielding drive to create a brighter future for myself.

As we move deeper into this thrift store of my life, remember that each item is not just a piece of junk; it's a fragment of my soul, a bit of my story, a part of my journey. Each object is a silent witness to the battles fought, the wars won, and the victories achieved. It's a reminder of the strength within, the power of the human spirit, and the soul's resilience.

Over the years, this pattern of story creation continued. The narratives became more elaborate each time, the blame heavier, and my understanding of reality murkier. It was like living in an episode of Black Mirror, where nothing was quite as it seemed.

That's what living in a world scripted by someone else is like. You start questioning your perception. You start doubting your own truths. And most importantly, you start wondering whether there's any way out of this distorted reality show.

You see, my mother's narratives weren't limited to just holiday occasions. They were an evergreen feature of my life, popping up like unwanted ads on a smartphone app. From missing pots to school lunches, her narrative machine knew no limits.

An old, rusted-out lunchbox is next in this chaotic kaleidoscope of my past. It's seen better days, like my childhood. This lunchbox here has stories that make the second grade sound like an espionage thriller, where lunch ladies are secret agents and lunchboxes hold state secrets.

So, here's the scene. Young me, coming back home from school, expecting maybe a cookie or, I don't know, a hug? Nah, what I got was my mom with that look in her eye and the "I know what you did" tone of voice. Seriously, I was just hoping for bagel bites.

"*Really? Throwing away the lunches I pack for you?*" she snapped. If looks could kill, I'd be six feet under.

"*What? I'm eating them! I really am!*" I replied, my small voice trembling against her onslaught.

"*Oh, so the lunch lady's a liar now?*"

This lunchbox here? It has scars from the battle of unbelieved truths and imaginary lunch lady informants. It's like a metallic veteran of Mom's war on reality.

"*Mom, I promise I never throw my lunch away!*" My protests were whispers in the hurricane of her wrath.

Reality was a visitor my mom rarely entertained. In her world, an imaginary lunch lady's made-up tales weighed more than her son's tears and pain. The arguments and screams were like bee stings on my young heart. Wooden spoons and paint stirrers were the weaponry of her rage, leaving wounds inside and out.

"*Ungrateful!*" she spat, throwing me repeatedly into the kitchen cabinets like a rag doll for what felt like hours.

This lunchbox silently witnessed the hunger that followed, the days without sandwiches or lunch money. I had to constantly depend on others for sustenance, but I felt the desire for normalcy, for a mother who nurtured instead of neglected.

There's a sort of bitter comedy in the whole ordeal. The very agents of my mother's ludicrous tales became my saviors. The lunch ladies, the supposed spies in Mom's web of conspiracies, became my closest pals. It's like befriending the secret agents in a weird, twisted spy movie. I was just this kid navigating the wild, tumultuous seas of elementary school, and the agents of lunch were my anchor.

"*Hey, sweetie, you want these extra fries?*" They'd whisper, sneaking me little bits of this and that as if we were exchanging top-secret intel.

"*I got a spare sandwich. You want it?*" another would wink, sliding me the contraband across the counter.

These kind, big-hearted women saw a kid in need and reached out, lending me a hand in my mom-induced turmoil. Their acts of kindness, whispered words, and smuggled sandwiches were like rays of sunshine in my grey world. It's funny. I'd never thought a stealthily passed chicken sandwich could feel like a hug, but it did.

High school came around, and boy, did I hatch a master plan. I got myself a job in the school cafeteria. It was a smart move. It was like being an inside man. Not only did it get me a paycheck, but it also meant free lunch. Yes, Free

Lunch! It was like hitting the jackpot in the casino of life. It was about surviving and getting by in the world where my mother had left me to fend for myself.

Every day, clad in that glamorous apron, I'd watch the swarms of teenagers buzzing around, engulfed in their adolescent dramas, oblivious to the silent battles being fought in the shadows. And there I was, behind the counter, a quiet warrior armed with a serving spoon, fighting his own war.

It wasn't just about the food, though. It was about belonging, about finding a place in a world that seemed determined to push me out. With their warm smiles and smuggled sandwiches, those lunch ladies were like a makeshift family, a band of merry rebels in the war against hunger and loneliness.

Every clandestine extra scoop of mac' n' cheese, every secretively passed piece of fruit, was a symbol, a beacon of humanity in a world overshadowed by the dark clouds of my mother's twisted games. The universe told me, "Kid, you are not alone. *You are seen. You are worth the extra scoop of mashed potatoes.*"

I'd immerse myself in conversations, sharing laughs over burnt pizzas and spilled milk. It was a sanctuary where I was just another teenager, not the boy with the twisted mother, not the child with the shattered innocence. It was a place where I was seen, where I was heard, where I mattered.

Through the clatter of trays and the hum of adolescent chatter in the heart of that busy cafeteria, I found solace, acceptance, and fragments of the love I was starved of. And amidst the aroma of baked beans and the warmth of freshly baked bread, I felt a sense of belonging, a feeling of being a part of something greater than my pain, more significant than my past.

This cafeteria, with its whispers of secret kindness, is like a beacon in the chaotic tapestry of my life, a reminder of the goodness lurking in unexpected corners. Let's keep moving, exploring more artifacts of my journey.

Despite the hurt and confusion, I clung to one thing: the truth. The narratives my mother spun were disorienting. They were meant to manipulate, to assert control, to gaslight. They were her attempts to mold reality into a shape that satisfied her whims and insecurities.

In the throes of these delusions, I was the target. My mother's words were arrows, aiming to undermine my confidence and self-worth. But through it all, I held on. I held onto the knowledge that I was not a thief, not a liar, not the ungrateful child she painted me to be. I knew my own heart, my own actions. I knew that the boy who loved to laugh, dreamed of being a superstar, and wished to be seen and loved by his own mother was not the monster she portrayed.

Holding onto my truth became my act of rebellion, my silent defiance. It was me saying, "I see what you're doing, and I won't let it define me." It was an act of self-preservation, an assertion of my identity in the face of her continuous attempts to distort it. But it was also a heavy burden for a child to bear. I had to grow up too quickly and put on an armor of resilience that no child should have to wear. My innocence was lost amid the battlefield of her narratives, replaced by a profound understanding of human manipulation and emotional cruelty.

The saving grace was that I discovered a strength I didn't think I had. A core of steel, wrapped in layers of soft humanity, weathering the storms she threw my way. It's something we all have hidden within us. A strength that enables us to endure, to persevere, and most importantly, to evolve. This strength allowed me to keep faith in the boy inside, to protect him (the best I could), and to assure him that he wasn't alone. And even when times were dark, that strength - my truth - was my beacon of light.

Remembering this, I realize we all have our inner lights flickering steadfastly in the winds of adversity. The hurt and confusion may try to snuff it out but hold onto it, guard it. That light, our truth, leads us out of the storm and into calmer seas.

Ok, one more thrift shop goodie. And this one, a pot? Picture it: It's Christmas day, my sophomore year in high school. The air outside was nippy, perfect for a cup of hot cocoa. It wasn't a usual thing; my mother hardly cooked. But this Christmas, she decided to turn into Martha Stewart.

As she rummaged through the kitchen for a specific pot to make the hot cocoa in, her mood changed from festive to furious. The pot she was searching for was nowhere to be found, and guess who was accused of a pot-related crime I didn't commit? That's right, yours truly. Suddenly, I was the rogue teen who'd made off with a pot, a plot twist even Hollywood screenwriters wouldn't dare to script. The missing pot became an excuse for a verbal onslaught and yet another example of my mother's wild narratives.

It's painful to revisit these memories. But it's important to remember that we aren't those scared, confused kids anymore. We're adults who can understand, process, and overcome the narratives we were forced into. We've grown, and that, my friends, is worth celebrating. As much as my mother's narratives formed the storm clouds of my childhood, they didn't define me. They shaped me, for sure. But they don't dictate my future, identity, or worth. That, my friends, was all up to me.

One of the most scarring memories was during high school, a period of self-discovery and finding one's place. Preparing for my show choir audition, I poured my heart into every note, every pitch. The shrill of her laughter from upstairs, mocking me, pierced through the melodious hum.

"What are you doing down there?" she'd tease.

Each snicker was a dagger to my dreams, clipping the wings of my aspirations, one feather at a time. Despite her shadow, my school became my refuge. I poured my heart into performing arts, hoping the applause and adoration from the crowd would fill the void she left behind. And, for brief moments, they did. They made me forget her giggles during my rehearsals or her claims that I'd only make it big as a Christian singer. Whatever that means.

Then, Senior year came—a monumental time in any teenager's life. It was the last year of high school, the edge of independence, and the cusp of adulthood. I landed the role of Conrad Birdie in "Bye Bye Birdie." I was ecstatic. Months of rehearsal, vocal training, and choreography practice led to the opening night. The lights dimmed, the audience settled, and the orchestra began its overture. My heart raced, filled with anticipation. As Conrad Birdie, I was no longer the boy with the chaotic home life. Instead, I was the heartthrob pop star of the 1960s, dazzling audiences and stirring emotions. But during the opening performance, a familiar, unwelcome sight caught my eye. My mother, late as usual, stumbled in, guided by her tipsy best friend to the front row. They giggled and fumbled, drawing the eyes of the entire theater towards them. I wanted to crawl into a hole, but the show had to go on. Each song, each dance step, became a battle to ignore her and remain in character.

The applause at the end of the show was thunderous. Friends, teachers, and acquaintances raved about the performance. The curtain calls were a blur of emotions—pride in the show, frustration at my mother, relief that it was over. However, underneath it all was the gnawing reminder that the place that gave me joy and refuge was invaded by the person I wished to escape from the most.

Despite the highs and lows of high school and the constant emotional turmoil, there was a silver lining. Friends who stood by my side, teachers who believed in me, and mentors who saw beyond my home situation and encouraged me to chase my dreams. Their support was a beacon, guiding me through the darkest storms and reminding me that a shore was waiting for me beyond the tumultuous waves—a place of peace, acceptance, and genuine love.

The story would only be complete with my coming out story. You know something you do in your own time, in your own way. The day began like any other, with sunlight streaming through the gaps in the blinds and the familiar hum of life outside. But what was to follow would be far from ordinary, forever marking itself in my memory.

In my room, lost in my thoughts, a sudden scream pierced the stillness, echoing with a venom I had never heard before. My mother's voice was loaded with a potent mix of fury and disbelief. She had stumbled upon the secret I had guarded so fiercely. Before I could muster a response, she was upon me, her words sharp, cutting through the atmosphere like shards of glass. Each name, each insult, landed like a blow. Her spit, a symbol of her disdain, marked me.

"*You should be eating a pussy and not sucking on a dick, you faggot!*" my mother screamed before storming up the stairs. As suddenly as she stormed in, she stormed out, tires screeching against the asphalt as she sped off.

Minutes turned to hours, though it felt like an eternity. I was left grappling with the avalanche of emotions her outburst had buried me under. Then, as dusk settled, the roar of the car's engine announced her return. Yet, it wasn't the mother I knew who came back. This woman clutched two large 40-ounce beers and a pack of Virginia Slim Menthol Ultra Lights, emblems of her desire to drown out reality, to escape from the truth she had just confronted. The back porch became her stage. As she cracked open a beer, she started her tirade anew, amplified by the telephone in her hand. She dialed number after number, recounting her discovery to anyone who would listen, embellishing it with her toxic mix of disdain and gossip. Every word she spoke was like an arrow aimed straight at me, and I was pinned, defenseless, listening to her describe me in ways that were far from who I was.

Yet, the ordeal was far from over. Marching back inside, she commanded, no, demanded that I call my father. "Tell him," she hissed, pushing the phone into my hands. My fingers trembled as I dialed, anxiety knotting my stomach. But his voice, warm and confused, was a balm. He didn't understand or comprehend why she was making me do this, but his acceptance shone through.

If only the night had ended there. But when she discovered I had a boyfriend, it fueled her fiery rage. Without a second thought, she was on the phone again, determined to drag more people into our private hell, creating drama where none was needed. In her tempest of emotion, one beacon of hope was my younger brother. Amidst her chaos, he stood as a pillar of support, his simple embrace conveying a message more powerful than words. "*I love you. You're still my brother.*"

That day was a testament to the extremes of human emotion, from the depths of cruelty to the peaks of conditional love. While she tried her best to belittle me, to crush my spirit, the love and acceptance of those who truly mattered ensured that I wasn't broken. They gave me the strength to rise above her storm and to find my own path to self-acceptance and love. I want to make something clear. Yes, those narratives, those storms—they left their mark. They shaped how I view the world, how I interact with people, and even how I view myself. They formed the lens through which I initially perceived reality—a lens clouded by distortions and false accusations. But lenses can be changed, views can be adjusted, and perceptions can evolve.

You see, those narratives were forced upon me. I didn't choose them; they were thrust onto my young, impressionable self. They were the shackles I wore for a considerable part of my life. But as I grew older, I realized something. I am not the reflection of my mother's distorted stories. I am not a character in her chaotic play. I am my own person with my own story to write. I decided not to let her narratives chart the course of my life. The decision wasn't easy; it was like standing at the edge of a cliff, the old familiar path behind me and the open sky ahead. It required courage, strength, and a lot of faith in myself. But the moment I made that leap and chose myself over her narratives, the change was exhilarating.

That's when I realized that my worth is not defined by the accusations and the beatings. It's not measured by the narratives woven by someone else. My value is determined by my resilience, ability to overcome the odds, and capacity to love and forgive in the face of hate and harm.

The identity I carved for myself is a testament to my strength and perseverance. I shaped my future, where I choose kindness over bitterness, understanding over judgment, and love over resentment. My identity is that of a survivor, a fighter, a person who can stand in the face of a storm and come out stronger. And the beauty of it all? This power, this control over our future and identity, is not exclusive to me. You have it, too. It resides within you, waiting to be discovered and unleashed.

As we reach the end of this emotional tour of my rollercoaster childhood, we've waded through the ups, downs, and loop-de-loops of living in a world scripted by someone else. You might have found a reflection of your own experiences in mine or felt the chilling familiarity of shared trauma.

Remember, as we dust off these memories, we're not here to wallow in sorrow. No, we're here to find solace, strength, and a bit of humor in shared experiences. As tumultuous as it was, my childhood did not define me. I carried a treasure chest of resilience, and so do you. I found the courage to hold on to my truth amid all the fiction. And if you're still holding onto yours or just beginning to uncover it, congratulations! You're stronger than you realize.

Take a deep breath because the next part of our journey is about to begin. We've combed through the past, but now it's time to step into the present, where the real healing begins.

In the following chapters, we'll delve deeper into how we can take control of our narrative, break free from the chains of the past, and embrace our true selves. Because at the end of the day, we are not just products of our history but architects of our future. We will focus on the awakening process and talk about recognizing the patterns, the signs of abuse, and neglect. We'll unpack the survival tactics we adopted as children and begin to replace them with healthier coping mechanisms. We'll venture out of the shadow of others' narratives and step into the light of our own truth.

Take this transition as your own personal intermission. Stretch a little, hydrate, and prepare yourself for the empowering journey of recognition. And remember, no matter how bumpy the road gets, we'll navigate it together.

CHAPTER 3

BEHIND CLOSED DOORS: UNDERSTANDING THE PROBLEM

Parental neglect and abuse are a bit like a Darth Vader moment - heavy on the breathing and dark side, light on the fatherly love. Now, parental neglect and abuse come in many forms, like *Pokémon*, only you don't really want to catch 'em all. Or any, for that matter. For some, neglect might be a parent being too busy to listen or take an interest in their lives. For others, it might be a parent who's physically present but emotionally as distant as Pluto.

This neglect can take many forms. Neglect might take the form of a parent being too absorbed in their own world to listen or take an interest in your life. Neglect can often feel like trying to converse with someone constantly scrolling through their phone - you know they're physically present, but mentally, they might as well be in Narnia.

Emotionally, neglectful parents might forget important dates, ignore your feelings, or never quite meet your gaze. It's like being ghosted, only it's happening within your home by the people who should have your back. The isolation from this neglect can be as cold as a winter in Siberia, making you feel more like an accessory in their lives than a protagonist in your own story.

The worst part? This neglect is often brushed off as the parent being 'busy'. It's concealed beneath excuses and justifications like a bad reality show hidden behind a glossy, glamorous trailer. But let me tell you something - genuine care and interest must be supported by busyness. Love finds a way to express itself.

The impact of this subtle, pervasive neglect can be far-reaching and long-lasting. It's like a slow water drip - it can erode even the hardest of stones over time. For a child, this consistent lack of parental interest can leave an indelible mark on their sense of self-worth and esteem, shaping how they see themselves and the world around them.

Remember, neglect and abuse aren't always loud - they're not just the dragons and legendary *Pokémon* of your childhood journey. They can also be the silent Dittos and Abra that disappear when you try to confront them. But no matter how they manifest, it's important to remember that it's not your fault.

And then, of course, there's abuse, which can take many forms - physical, emotional, or verbal. Think of it like the different kinds of jellybeans in Bertie Bott's Every Flavor Beans pack - the ones from *Harry Potter* that include all sorts of wild flavors. But unlike finding the occasional vomit-flavored jellybean (no thank you, Bertie), this is more like each one packs a punch that leaves a lingering sour taste. Imagine you're holding a box of those beans - Except in our unfortunate version of this magical candy, each jellybean represents a different form of parental abuse. It's a metaphor, albeit a pretty grim one.

Physical abuse is like unexpectedly biting into a hot chili-flavored jellybean when your taste buds are fully prepared for cherry. It's a jarring shock to your system that feels like it's coming from out of left field. You were anticipating sweetness a moment before, and now you're left grappling with an inferno in your mouth.

This brutal form of abuse can take many shapes and forms - hitting, slapping, pushing, or any other action designed to inflict physical harm. These hurtful acts burn and sting, creating immediate pain and a lingering aftermath of suffering. It's a twofold trauma. On the one hand, you have the physical hurt that imprints on your body, the apparent marks that may fade with time but never truly disappear. Then, on the other hand, there's the invisible pain - the betrayal, the confusion, the fear that simmers long after the physical wounds have healed, kind of like the lingering burn on your tongue from that nasty chili jellybean.

This is the real, double-edged sword of physical abuse. It's not just the visceral pain that leaves you reeling; it's that betrayal that leaves you questioning everything you thought you knew. It's the realization that the person who should have been your refuge has become a source of your fear. It's a tough pill to swallow, way more brutal than any chili jellybean, but it's essential to understanding the pervasive damage caused by physical abuse. And it's a necessary step on the path toward healing.

Sometimes, the physical signs aren't obvious, like a vast red welt on your forehead. They can be subtle, like hidden Easter Eggs in a Pixar movie - a grip that's too tight, a forceful shove, or a pose that's uncomfortable to hold for too long. These tiny, cumulative moments of hurt often go unseen but are felt all too deeply.

And it's not just about the dodgeball hitting you; it's the chaos it causes inside your head. You start thinking it's your fault for not dodging fast enough, that maybe you did something to deserve this. It's a messed-up game where the rules don't make sense, and you're always getting hit.

As we all know from watching Disney movies, the bad stuff doesn't just disappear when the credits roll. Physical abuse can morph into an ugly hydra, spawning heads of anxiety, depression, and even PTSD. It's like carrying a knapsack full of Horcruxes; it weighs you down, even if you can't see it.

Imagine trying to play a simple, joyous game of hopscotch. You should be concentrating on hopping from square to square, enjoying the rhythm of the game, feeling the breeze on your face, and maybe the laughter of friends ringing in your ears. Now, replace the harmless chalk squares with volatile landmines. Suddenly, the simple childhood game is no longer a game - it's a life-threatening obstacle course. You're constantly alert, your heart pounding in your chest, your mind racing with fear and worry. The laughter is replaced by a deafening silence, punctuated only by your shallow breaths.

This is what it's like for a child living in a physically abusive home. The usual innocence of childhood is lost, replaced with constant fear and vigilance. You're always looking for signs of the following violent outburst, like scanning the ground for the next landmine. In this environment, the everyday aspects of childhood often get neglected. Concentrating on algebra is hard when you're more worried about avoiding a beating after school. Friendships are harder to maintain when you're too embarrassed or scared to invite anyone home. As for Saturday morning cartoons, they can become a luxury - a slice of normalcy that feels out of reach when you're living in survival mode.

What should be a time of learning, growth, and exploration becomes a harrowing exercise in survival. You learn to walk on eggshells, trying to avoid setting off the subsequent explosion, and in doing so, a significant part of your childhood gets lost in the minefield. But it's crucial to remember that this minefield is not the whole world. Beyond it lies a vast landscape of healing and possibilities; together, we will navigate our way toward it. Step by cautious step.

Next up to the stage is **Emotional Abuse** - she can be as subtle and complex to pin down as those weird, ambiguous flavors - you know, the one that might be grass or green apple? You're just not sure.

Emotional abuse might involve constant criticism, humiliation, dismissiveness, or manipulation. It's often hard to spot, but just like a grass-flavored jellybean in a mouthful of fruit flavors, it leaves a noticeable taste of 'wrong' that lingers long after the initial bite.

Emotional abuse, sometimes known as *psychological abuse*, is the masked villain of the abuse family. It's like a chameleon, blending into the background, making it hard to pin down. Emotional abuse is all about power and control, just like how Voldemort controlled his Death Eaters. However, unlike He-Who-Must-Not-Be-Named, emotional abuse often has no physical or visible mark. It's the snide remark that chips away at your confidence, the cruel joke that's always at your expense, and the public humiliation that feels like a Dementor's kiss to your self-esteem. In the family setting, emotional abuse can manifest in various ways. Emotional abuse can be constant criticism, dismissiveness, manipulation, and humiliation.

Let's imagine for a second that every little victory, every A+ on your math test, and every pat on the back is like building a kick-ass sandcastle. Like the ones you spend all day making at the beach, getting the towers just right? Yeah, those ones.

Now, imagine whenever you've got that tower standing tall and proud, someone kicks it down, nonchalantly muttering, "Meh, you could have done better." That's the life when you're living under a constant rain of criticism. It's like having your personal rain cloud following you around, drenching every happy moment.

Being constantly critiqued is like having your own personal critic, whispering sweet nothings like, "Nice try, but not quite there." And you know what? When this kind of crap happens within the family, it hurts. It's like a low blow every single time.

Living with constant criticism it's like trying to keep your balance on a tightrope. You're wobbling, trying to get to the other side, but each word, each jab, is like a gust of wind trying to knock you off. It's exhausting, it's disheartening. It makes you question your worth and your abilities. You could be building the Taj Mahal, and all you'd hear is, "Is this the best you can do?"

When your family, the people who are supposed to be your cheerleaders, become your critics, it's a new level of betrayal. Every achievement is overshadowed by a looming "but," and every success is undermined by a whispered "if only." You find yourself constantly in the shadow of what could have been, always reminded of what you supposedly lack.

Then there is dismissiveness. It's like being the main character in your episode of *The Twilight Zone*. Everyone around you seems to be speaking some foreign, outlandish language, and no matter how hard you try, how loudly you scream, how clearly you enunciate... your words, your feelings—they're like whispers in a storm, completely and utterly lost in translation.

Picture this: it's like you're shouting, screaming from the top of your lungs, but all that comes out are inaudible squeaks like a human dog whistle. And your feelings and thoughts are like bubbles in the wind, visible for a split second before they pop into nothingness. You know they're real. You feel them, live them, but to the world around you, they might as well not exist. It's like screaming into the void and expecting an echo, but all you get is silence. It's like being a ghost in your own life, wandering around, trying to communicate, to connect, but all your attempts pass through, leaving you increasingly frustrated and more invisible. Every dismissed thought, every invalidated feeling, it's like another layer of you fades away until you start to wonder if you're real or just a figment of your imagination.

It's an isolating, frustrating experience, making you feel trapped in a box where your screams bounce off the walls, unheard by anyone else. It's living in a world where your feelings are treated like unwanted guests, quickly shown the door before they can even sit down.

You start to question your own reality, your sanity. "Am I just overreacting? Am I the crazy one here?" It's like living in a fog of doubt and uncertainty, where every step forward feels like a step into the unknown. It's a constant battle between wanting to be heard and the fear of being invalidated repeatedly.

Imagine all this wrapped up in the daily grind of life, coupled with the constant, lingering ghost of your past, haunting every step, whispering sweet nothings of self-doubt and fear. It's like a relentless game of hide and seek where you're always "it," constantly searching but never finding.

Every dismissive word, every invalidated feeling, is like a small cut, slowly bleeding you out, draining the color from your world, leaving everything in varying shades of grey. You start to live in this monochromatic world, where joy is just a distant memory, and pain is your constant companion.

The worst part, the absolute kicker? It makes you dismissive of yourself, makes you invalidate your own feelings, makes you echo the words of those around you until their voice becomes your voice, and their dismissiveness becomes your dismissiveness. It's like a twisted, self-fulfilling prophecy where you become the architect of your misery.

Let's remember manipulation, that sneaky, snaky thing. It's the invisible maestro of emotional abuse. It's like you're stuck with a real-life Geppetto, but unlike the kind-hearted puppet maker, this one's not interested in crafting a lovable wooden child. Nope. This one's busy carving, twisting, and reshaping your reality to fit into their warped storytelling.

Imagine living where every single day, your truth and your feelings are like Play-Doh in the hands of a toddler—mashed, molded, and mushed to look like their crazy version of the world. It's not about creating a pretty picture. It's about warping your world until it's a wacky, wonky reflection of their deranged desires.

And this puppet master? Oh, they know exactly which strings to pull, which levers to toggle to turn you into their personal marionette, leaving you swirling in a whirlpool of confusion and chaos. It's like being stuck in a funhouse full of twisted, stretching mirrors—each reflection a distorted mockery of reality.

The real pain? It's the continuous doubting, the constant questioning tearing you from the inside, whispering shadows of distortion, making you dance to their whims. It's not the vivid, loud pain of the overt abuses but the silent, creeping shadow, which slowly wraps its fingers around you, choking your essence bit by bit. The struggle? That's in reclaiming your truth from this maze of distortions. It's about breaking the strings, stepping out of the shadows, and saying,

"Enough! This is MY truth, MY reality!"

47

Now here's the granddaddy of them all: *Humiliation*. Humiliation? Oh, it's like being in the middle of a roast. Except you never signed up for it, and there is no chance for a rebuttal. It's having your flaws, insecurities, and private matters thrown into the spotlight and then dissected, magnified, and mocked. It's like being the punchline to a joke that everyone but you finds amusing.

The public embarrassment—it's not a hushed whisper. It's a loudspeaker announcement to the world, disclosing your flaws and mishaps. It's like standing naked in a crowd, feeling a thousand eyes pierce through you, each gaze an icy dagger. It's being strung up like a puppet, yanked and jerked around. It's dancing, but not to a tune you like—it's more like a cacophony of your insecurities and fears being played on a loop. It's a constant reminder of your 'place'— somewhere below, where laughter is the cruel ruler and shadows are your constant companions.

Here's where the irony comes in; this is not just humiliation. It's degradation wrapped up in shiny paper and a bow—a gift that keeps giving. It's the daily reminder that you're just the jester, the fool, the comedic relief in the tragic play of life.

Finally, there's **Verbal Abuse**; let me tell you, it's no less damaging. Picture the vomit-flavored jellybean. Yeah, that's right - Bertie really went there. Verbal abuse might involve shouting, threats, or belittling comments that are as enjoyable as that revolting flavor in your mouth. This abuse can be as harmful as physical abuse, undermining self-esteem and leading to long-term psychological harm.

Verbal abuse doesn't leave any physical marks, but trust me, it hurts. Think of it like an unexpected sour note in your favorite song - it's jarring and unpredictable and ruins the whole melody. It might come in the form of shouting like a speaker turned up too loud, distorting all the sound. Or it's threats, which hang over your head like a storm cloud, ready to rain on your parade at any moment. It could also be belittling comments, those sneaky little digs that chip away at your self-esteem like a woodpecker on a tree trunk.

Just because you can't see the damage, doesn't mean it's not there. Verbal abuse can undermine your self-esteem faster than a deflating balloon, leaving you feeling flat and empty. It can lead to long-term psychological harm, casting a long, cold shadow over your sense of self-worth. But you know what? Identifying this kind of abuse is the first step toward healing. It's like recognizing that you've been eating spoiled food all along - it's a tough pill to swallow, but it's necessary for your health.

What's important to remember is that, just like you didn't choose the flavors in the candy box, no person chooses to be on the receiving end of abuse. It's thrust upon them, leaving them to deal with the unpleasant aftermath. But here's the thing - unlike that box of jellybeans, the effects of abuse aren't as easy to wash away with a quick drink of water.

We'll explore these forms of abuse more throughout the book, alongside strategies for coping, healing, and, most importantly, moving forward. As grim as the jellybean analogy is, I promise sweeter flavors are ahead.

Now, let's talk about the elephant in the room: **Narcissism**. Not the healthy self-esteem kind, but the personality disorder that can turn parents into real-life versions of the Evil Queen from *Snow White*. You know, the ones who always ask for validation from a mirror because they have an insatiable need to be the fairest.

A narcissistic parent is often self-absorbed, manipulative, and lacks empathy. It's like living with a less cool version of a comic book supervillain - all the mind games, none of the rad powers. They can be so preoccupied with their desires and feelings that they forget their child's needs.

Picture a real-life version of Gaston from *Beauty and the Beast* - minus the killer biceps and catchy theme song. They're so focused on their reflection in the mirror, so bewitched by their charm, that they can't look away and notice anyone else's needs. Like, hello? Other people exist, too!

Oh and how they love to manipulate. Just like every Disney movie villain who tricks the hero with a cunning plan, only to reveal their true colors at the climax? That's the narcissistic parent - except there's no cheerful singing and dancing to lighten the mood. They can twist and turn every situation to make it about themselves, and suddenly, you're stuck in a web of guilt and obligation.

A narcissistic parent's lack of empathy is like living with a dementor from *Harry Potter's* world. They suck out all the joy and leave you feeling cold and empty. They're so wrapped up in their own world that they forget their primary role - being a parent. Imagine if Luke Skywalker's story was all about Darth Vader's drama, and no one bothered to ask Luke how he felt about having his hand chopped off. That's what it's like - you're sidelined in your life story.

Just like our favorite movie heroes, we're not doomed to remain stuck in these loops. Understanding is the first step towards change, and I promise you, we've got plenty of steps to go. Let us remember the survival mode many fall into due to these issues. It's a phrase you've probably heard concerning finals week in college or when you had to assemble IKEA furniture with nothing but a tiny hex key and your undying will.

However, in the context of growing up with parental neglect or abuse, survival mode is less about making it through a stress-packed week and more about living every single day in a state of hyper-awareness, always waiting for the other shoe to drop. Survival mode is like being stuck in the green pipe underworld of a *Super Mario* game - it's a dark, unfamiliar place where you're constantly on edge, dodging the Goombas and Koopa Troopas that life throws at you.

You know the bit I'm talking about – the underground levels. The music gets ominous, the lovable blue sky is replaced by claustrophobic brick, and your path is suddenly riddled with all sorts of hazards. Goombas are creeping around, deadly to the touch. Koopa Troopas are bouncing around like they've had too much caffeine, and don't even get me started on the Piranha Plants. The bottom line is it's not a fun place to be. And you're there without any power-ups.

This might translate to always being on high alert and trying to anticipate your parent's moods to avoid confrontation. It could mean suppressing your needs or feelings to prevent potential outbursts or make yourself less noticeable. It's like being in a constant fight, flight, or freeze response.

And here's the thing about the *Super Mario* underworld analogy: those levels are temporary. Mario eventually emerges into daylight and goes about his cheerful, princess-saving journey. But when you're a child stuck in survival mode due to ongoing neglect or abuse, it can feel like you're permanently stuck in that dark, danger-filled underworld. You grow up too fast, taking on responsibilities and emotional burdens that no child should shoulder. It's like you're playing the game on hard mode while everyone else seems to have the cheat codes.

Survival mode, just like those underground levels, is different from where you want to stay. You deserve to reach those bright, sun-filled levels where the coin blocks are plentiful, and the most significant threat is a goofy turtle who can't seem to keep track of his princess. And that's where we're heading – towards the daylight, towards healing. The underworld levels are challenging, but every good gamer knows they're just a path to something better.

So, there you have it. We've taken a tour through the not-so-merry land of abuse, which, to be honest, is about as fun as a ride on a broken roller coaster. We've stared down the gnarly face of physical abuse, grappled with the elusive specter of emotional abuse, and braced against the harsh winds of verbal abuse. These experiences, as we've discussed, can leave scars more profound and intricate than any physical wound. They seep into your psyche, color your worldview, and have you believing things about yourself that are as true as the idea of flying pigs.

But, as we've reached the end of this chapter, let's not forget the key message here: recognizing these forms of abuse is the first, crucial step towards healing. It's about acknowledging that you've walked through some pretty dark valleys, but those valleys don't define you. You're not a product of the negativity thrown at you. You're not the hurtful words yelled at you. You're not the dismissive attitude that belittled you. And you're certainly not the physical pain inflicted upon you.

You're so much more than all of that.

Remember, your past might have shaped you, but it doesn't own you. You're the driver in this journey, capable of steering your life towards brighter horizons. You're a lot stronger than you think, and I'm here with you to help guide you through it. As we journey onward, we will address how to heal, grow, and re-write our narratives to be a tale of resilience, recovery, and reclaiming our self-worth. So stick around, and keep those seatbelts fastened because this ride's only starting.

CHAPTER 4

THE CYCLE OF ABUSE

"Ah, the circle of life," I mused one day, mentally cueing Elton John's legendary vocals from *The Lion King*. I quickly realized that I was caught in less "Disney's Circle of Life" and more "Stephen King's Circle of Abuse."

The mental image of a sun-drenched Simba gave way to a somewhat less enchanting picture of a generational carousel spinning in a toxic cycle. It was an amusement park ride I'd been on far too long, and I felt dizzy.

Understanding the cycle of abuse and neglect is not as simple as explaining why Lindsay Lohan's music career never took off (no shade, Lindsay, I jammed to your albums...still do). Unfortunately, it's a complex and deeply rooted pattern that echoes through generations.

I was trapped in this cycle for most of my life. Mom, while she might've been a mean girl to give Regina George a run for her money, was herself a victim of this cycle, and her mother before her. It's a lot like that *Harry Potter* mirror that shows you your heart's desire, except all you see is a reflection of trauma staring back. I was living in a literal nightmare of "like mother, like son" - only in this case, I was not thrilled about the family resemblance.

One risk of this nasty merry-go-round is that you can unintentionally repeat these patterns in your relationships or, Gaga forbid, with your own children. It's like when you accidentally use a phrase your parents always said that you swore you'd never say. This isn't about innocently saying "because I said so," but more dangerous habits like manipulation, control, or neglect.

The thing about patterns is that they're comfortable in a twisted way, like a moth-eaten childhood blanket. We know them, we understand them, and we've practiced them for years. Changing them feels like trying to write with your non-dominant hand while roller skating backward – it's awkward, feels unnatural, and you're likely to fall on your ass a few times.

Just like learning to use chopsticks, breaking the cycle of abuse is a skill. It requires practice, patience, and persistence. Trust me, I've been there, done that, and lived to write this book. The cycle can be broken, and I'm here to show you how. We're about to journey into the dark side of the moon, a deep dive into the nitty-gritty of the cycle of abuse and how to break free. Buckle up because it's gonna be a bumpy yet worthwhile ride. But hey, what road to redemption isn't?

This carousel of chaos typically starts with the *tension-building stage*. For me, it was like the ominous soundtracks in horror movies that signal the approach of a monster. But this monster was always invisible, living inside my mom.

Take, for instance, that fateful day when Mom couldn't find her favorite pot to make hot cocoa. I'd seen her agitation brewing like an ominous storm cloud, ready to unleash a torrential downpour. And boy, did it pour. Her rage splashed onto me, drenching me in the blame for a lost pot I knew nothing about. Think less "cozy Christmas story around the fireplace" and more "a nerve-wracking episode of Kitchen Nightmares."

Next comes the *incident*, or *acute explosion*. In my case, the blast was as literal as it gets, with wooden spoons and paint stirrers used as weapons. I sometimes felt like a pinball in the world's worst arcade game, bouncing off kitchen cabinets under the force of my mother's fury.

These explosions weren't your typical mother-son arguments, no. This was the stuff that would make a *Jerry Springer* episode seem like a Disney movie. Imagine entering a war zone where all the rules of engagement are thrown out the window, and the opposing side has all the firepower.

I was left defenseless against the torrent of words, accusations, and physical attacks, like that second-grade day when I came home from school, expecting to do some homework or watch cartoons. Instead, I was accused of throwing away my lunches and subjected to a punishment that would have made a medieval torturer flinch. I was thrown around like trash, headfirst into the cabinets, over and over. The kitchen became a war zone, and my childhood innocence was the casualty.

These experiences molded me into the anxious mess I became. One wrong move, one minor mistake, and boom! Emotional shrapnel everywhere. Each attack chipped away at my self-esteem, sense of security, and belief in a world where parents are supposed to protect their children, not harm them.

But you know what they say, "*What doesn't kill you gives you a dark sense of humor and a lot of material for a book.*" The absurdity of it all is apparent in retrospect: a child being held responsible for a missing pot or a fabricated lunch-throwing scandal. The scenarios sound ludicrous, and yet they were my reality.

The *Incident Stage* in an abusive cycle is the most visible one. We can point to it and say, "*That was wrong. That was abuse.*" But it also confuses us the most, especially when we're still inside the cycle. It's when we ask ourselves, "*What did I do to deserve this?*" The answer, as I've learned, is absolutely nothing.

This stage often ends in remorse, or what some might call the *Honeymoon Phase*. It's a deceptive lull in the storm when the abuser might show regret or kindness. For me, it was the occasional Taco Bell dinner bought or my mom playing Nintendo with me, their rarity making them seem like treasures. These moments felt like the universe pressing the 'pause' button, giving me enough hope to make it through another cycle.

This so-called "*Honeymoon Phase*" can be as seductive as that extra guacamole at Chipotle—yes, you know it will cost you, but it's hard to resist. During these periods of calm, the abuser may show a side that you crave to see more of—kindness, remorse, maybe even love.

For a child starving for affection, a Nacho Supreme with no tomato might as well have been a five-course meal at a Michelin-starred restaurant. It wasn't about the food, really. It was about the illusion of normalcy, the tantalizing possibility of having a mother who cared about my happiness, even if it was through something as simple as fast food.

These moments were rare, but they immensely influenced my emotional landscape. Because, in those moments, my mom wasn't a rampaging Godzilla destroying everything in her path—she was, briefly, my mom. The one who'd take me out for tacos and laugh at my school stories.

But the catch with these moments—the avocado pit— was that they were fleeting and unpredictable. They were like getting a surprise celebrity cameo in the middle of a B-grade horror flick—you'd get a thrill, but it didn't change the fact you were still watching a terrible movie. And the worst part? These moments of "kindness" would fuel my hope. Hope that maybe this time, she'd changed. This time, we'd be like the families I saw on TV, where problems were resolved within a neat 30-minute episode, and everyone loved each other unconditionally.

Hope, like those Taco Bell trips, was a tricky beast. It gave me enough sustenance to endure another round of the abuse cycle, waiting for the next Nacho Supreme, the next hint of "kindness," the next pause in the storm. And so, without realizing it, I was caught in the cycle, tethered to the hope that the good moments would start outweighing the bad.

Recognizing this pattern was my first step towards breaking free. But to do that, I had to accept a hard truth: the occasional taco dinner wasn't enough. I deserved more. I deserved consistent love, respect, and kindness— not breadcrumbs of affection doled out between storms of abuse.

It's time we take off our rose-colored glasses and see these *honeymoon phases* for what they really are—a part of the cycle of abuse, not a respite from it. The road to healing begins with understanding, and that's exactly what we're here to do.

Finally, there's the calm before the storm or the *Reconciliation Phase*. But let's be clear: this isn't a kumbaya moment of healing and forgiveness. It's more like that eerie quiet in horror films where everyone (including you, the viewer) knows something else is about to go down.

When you're living in the eye of a cyclone of abuse, this calm phase can be confusing, misleading, and even a source of guilt. It's a masterclass in manipulation, distorting your perception of reality. My mother was a Picasso of this genre.

She could flip the switch from a wrathful deity to a remorseful sinner faster than a chameleon changes color. One moment, she was slinging hurtful words and objects around like a Greek god in a fit of rage, and the next, she would be simmering down, perhaps even turning kind or — dare I say it — maternal.

It was as if the storm had passed, and there was this temporary rainbow of peace and normalcy. These times were when my mother could almost pass for a Hallmark movie mom, offering me tiny glimpses of the motherly love I craved.

But as enticing as these moments were, they were also the breeding grounds for self-doubt. When you're constantly being spun around in the cyclone of abuse, these calm patches can make you question your judgment.

"Was it really that bad?"

"Am I overreacting?"

"Maybe she's changed."

These thoughts were my constant companions, always hovering in the back of my mind. It was like a sinister gaslighting choir singing a symphony of self-doubt. The truth is, though, these moments of calm were merely the veneer, the deceitful facade, the wizard behind the curtain. The storm was still there, just waiting to make its encore appearance. It was as predictable as a daytime soap opera's plot twist, yet it always caught me off-guard.

This stage of the cycle is perhaps the hardest to recognize because it's filled with hope. The abuser often behaves as if the abuse never happened or minimizes it. In my case, my mother was an expert in both. This is when you might think, "Maybe this time it's different," only to have your hopes dashed when the cycle inevitably begins again.

This is the danger of the calm before the storm. It's not a restful lull; it's the deceptive stillness that precedes the hurricane. Recognizing it for what it is can be a significant step toward breaking the cycle. Only when we see the storm for what it truly is can we begin to seek shelter.

Breaking this cycle can feel like trying to solve a Rubik's cube blindfolded while upside-down. It's not easy, and there are setbacks. Just like when I tried to do a juice cleanse, and on day three, I found myself in a McDonald's drive-through at midnight. (Don't judge, those fries and Diet Cokes are addictive!)

Healing requires you to unlearn years of conditioned responses to challenge everything you thought was "normal." It's like taking the red pill in *The Matrix* and suddenly realizing the world isn't what you thought it was. It's uncomfortable, it's challenging, and at times, it downright sucks. But let me tell you, it's also helpful. You see the world in a whole new light. You see yourself not as a victim but as a survivor, warrior, and hero in your epic saga.

Recognizing the cycle of abuse in your own life is a monumental task. Imagine for a second you're at a *Where's Waldo?* Convention. Everyone around you is clad in red and white stripes. And you are tasked with finding the real Waldo. It seems impossible at first. You're left feeling dizzy and confused with all those decoys and false alarms.

That's how it feels when you're deep in the cycle of abuse. The signs aren't always clear, especially when the person supposed to love and nurture you is causing the pain. You're swept up in this whirlwind of emotions, questioning your judgment and often blaming yourself for the chaos around you. The sea of candy cane-colored decoys represents the confusion, the deception, and the false narratives that are often part of an abusive dynamic. But then, something shifts. It could be a moment of clarity, or perhaps you've had enough, or someone else points it out for you. You may have read a book like this, heard a story like yours, and something clicked. You begin to connect the dots. You spot Waldo in the crowd.

Once you see the pattern—the tension building, the explosive incidents, the hollow remorse, the deceptive calm—it becomes a beacon, casting light on the darkest corners of your experiences. It's like turning on the lights in a room you've only ever seen in the dark. Suddenly, you see the cycle for what it is—a continuous loop of dysfunction and pain in which you've been entangled.

Recognizing these stages in your life can be painful. It's difficult to confront that your parent or loved one has been causing you harm. You might find yourself looking back at past incidents with fresh eyes, reassessing every interaction, every moment of conflict or calm. You may feel anger, sadness, guilt, or confusion. These feelings are valid and normal.

In all of this, remember that recognizing the pattern is not about blaming yourself. You're not responsible for someone else's abusive behavior. Instead, think of this as your path to understanding and healing. Seeing the cycle is the first step to breaking free from it.

On the battlefield of my childhood, the acute explosions were both the most violent and the most baffling. It took many years and lots of introspection to understand that these incidents were not my fault. I didn't ask for them and didn't deserve them. But here's the deal:

understanding is just the first step. It's what you do with that understanding that really counts.

You're probably asking now, "*How do we break free from this cycle?*" It's like asking, "*How do we stop a speeding train?*" It feels overwhelming and, at times, impossible. But guess what? It's not. With knowledge, support, and a stubborn refusal to be defined by our past, we can step off that train and onto a path that leads to healing.

The journey will be challenging. There may even be times when you'll want to turn back. But remember this: you're not alone. There's an entire community out here, myself included, who have walked this path before you and are cheering you on. Life might have given us lemons, but we'll make the best fucking lemonade you've ever tasted. And just so you know, the secret ingredient is resilience.

As we conclude this chapter, I leave you with this:

We are not the sum of the abuse we endured. We are not the scapegoats our abusive parents tried to make us. We are survivors, warriors, and ultimately, authors of our stories. And let me tell you, friends, our stories are just beginning.

CHAPTER 5

I SAW THE SIGN

F rom the outside looking in, my childhood might've appeared like a vintage film reel, full of nostalgia and simplicity. But for those of us in it, the film was more of a psychological thriller, complete with unpredictable plot twists and a lead character - my mother - who was as enigmatic as she was erratic.

As a child, I always knew something was off. Think of it like tuning into a radio station that's just slightly out of frequency - there's music, but it's all mixed with static and distortion. You might not understand what's wrong, but you can feel it in the pit of your stomach. Every child seeks love and validation from their parents, and I was no exception.

From a young age, I was cast in a supporting role in my mother's melodrama, navigating her stormy emotional landscapes with a child's determination and sensitivity far beyond my years. But it was a script I couldn't rewrite, no matter how hard I tried.

This wasn't the typical parent-child dynamic. Instead, it felt like walking on a tightrope over a chasm of unpredictable emotions. One misstep, one wrong word, and I'd tumble into a pit of her disapproval or anger. But the tightrope was my life, and I was determined to cross it, fueled by the hope that, eventually, I could find solid ground on the other side.

The revolving door of men in my mother's life added an extra layer of complexity to my already chaotic childhood. Each new man was like a shiny new distraction, a compelling plot twist in the Telenovela of her life. And when one of these "leading men" walked onto the stage, my brother and I were promptly pushed to the wings—out of sight and out of mind. Even though she constantly reminded us, she always puts her children first- one of her beautiful, narcissistic qualities.

I remember times when she would transform overnight from an indifferent, emotionally distant parent into a giddy schoolgirl. She'd spend hours preening in front of the mirror, making herself look just right for her next big date. Meanwhile, I would watch, my feelings a tangled knot of confusion, resentment, and hurt. It was as if our presence was an inconvenience, a reminder of a reality she'd rather forget.

In these moments, I became more of a parent than a child, yet amidst all this, a part of me still desperately yearned for my mother's love. I took on the role of her emotional caretaker, wiping away her tears after each heartbreak and listening to her woes. I'd buy her flowers and gifts with the money from my summer jobs, hoping these small acts of kindness would give me a moment in the spotlight of her affection.

This twisted dynamic was like being on a seesaw that was permanently weighted against me—no matter how hard I tried, I could never quite balance it out. But it wasn't until much later that I realized the simple, heart-wrenching truth: no child should have to buy their parent's love. Love should be the one constant in the seesaw of life, not something you earn or barter for.

Navigating the world as a child without a guiding hand or a loving gaze to reflect your worth is like being thrown into the pool's deep end without knowing how to swim. It's a sink-or-swim situation. But even amidst the chaos and the hurt, I was learning how to float. I was building resilience, and though I didn't know it then, I was gathering stories—ones that would later fuel my journey of healing and self-discovery.

Remember this, my friend: *we are not the sum of our childhood traumas.*

We are:
The strength that emerges from it.
The laughter that echoes despite it.
The love that persists beyond it.

This was her narrative, her script, and I was merely a character in her play. And no matter how hard I tried, no matter how many flowers I gave, how many tears I wiped, how many hurts I tried to heal, the script remained unchanged. The approval I sought was always out of reach, a mirage that would disappear whenever I thought I was close. It's like when you realize no superglue can fix your favorite coffee mug, shattered in pieces on the floor. It's heart-wrenching. It's unfair. It's a cold cup of reality being splashed in your face. Acknowledging that my mother couldn't be the loving figure I yearned for was a similar experience. It felt like I was mourning a loss, grieving for a person who never really existed.

But remember, dear reader, it's okay to grieve. Grieving isn't just about physical loss—it's also about acknowledging the loss of hopes, dreams, and expectations. I wept for the warm, nurturing mother-son bond I saw in movies and read in books. I grieved for the endless loop of "what could have been." And in doing so, I released myself from the tether of false hope that had kept me stuck in the cycle of abuse.

In this grieving process, I experienced a whole spectrum of emotions. Sadness, naturally, was a frequent visitor. I felt anger, too, at my mother for her actions and even at myself for the years I spent living in denial. I felt regret for the moments lost and time wasted. It was like navigating the five stages of grief, except instead of coming to terms with the death of a loved one, I was facing the harsh reality of an unfulfilled longing for a mother's love and care.

It's not an easy process, and the emotional turbulence can be overwhelming. It's like when Britney Spears shaved her head in 2007. It may have looked like a breakdown to the outside world, but it was a statement, an act of defiance, a woman exerting control in a life where she felt powerless.

My grieving process was similar—it was messy, it was public, and it was my way of taking control of my narrative. The world had seen me as a victim, a troubled kid, a rebel. But as I navigated my grief, I was writing my story, one where I was the hero, rising from the ashes.

Surrounding yourself with supportive, understanding people during this period is essential. This is where my husband stepped in like my personal cheerleader, always ready with a comforting hug or a well-timed joke to make me smile. Having someone who understands and validates your feelings can make the journey less isolating.

As you go through this process, remember this: Grieving is not a sign of weakness. It's not a flaw or a fault. It's a natural response to loss. And with abuse, it's an essential step in acknowledging your pain and starting your journey to healing. So let yourself grieve, let yourself feel, and let yourself heal. Because, in the immortal words of RuPaul, "*If you can't love yourself, how in the hell are you gonna love somebody else? Can I get an amen?*"

And then came the hard part—forging a new path. My healing journey wasn't about running from my past but understanding, accepting, and learning from it. And it wasn't about "fixing" myself either—I wasn't broken, but a survivor, strong and resilient. My journey was about discovery, growth, and, above all, self-love.

The path was filled with pitfalls and detours. Sometimes, I felt like I was walking on a tightrope, teetering between my past and future, healing and hurt. But every step was a victory, no matter how small or shaky. Each step took me further away from the toxicity of my past and closer to the healthy, thriving life I deserved.

There's a quote by the wickedly talented (cue John Travolta's mispronunciation from The 2014 Oscars) Idina Menzel, who once said, "It's not about perfection. It's about purpose." This journey isn't about creating a perfect life without pain or struggle. It's about living purposefully, finding your happiness, and, most importantly, learning to love yourself, even when it seems like the hardest thing to do.

Unfortunately, in my early life, I played out my mother's drama in my own love life, thinking that passion and pain were two sides of the same coin. I fought, yelled, and lashed out, all in the name of what I thought was love.

My romantic relationships were a reflection of the tumultuous dynamic I had with my mother, a mirror held up to the familial script I'd been reading for years. Unconsciously, I recreated the same drama, volatility, and manipulation patterns modeled for me during my formative years. In my world, love was a fierce storm, a rollercoaster of intense emotion that I mistook for passion.

Think about those epic, tragic love stories we've all watched unfold on the silver screen—Jack and Rose in *Titanic*, Edward and Bella in *Twilight*, or the passionate but tumultuous saga of Ross and Rachel in *Friends*. You know the type—high-stakes, high-drama, with a dose of heartache thrown into the mix. That's what I thought love was supposed to look like. It was supposed to hurt. The gut-wrenching pain of jealousy, insecurity, and betrayal—weren't these the markers of a love worth fighting for?

I found myself engaging in self-sabotaging behavior, picking fights, and pushing my partners away, only to reel them back in with apologies and promises of change. The push-pull dynamic was a whirlwind of confusion, hurt, and toxicity, but to me, it felt familiar. It felt like home. And in the worst possible way, it felt like love.

My relationships turned into a kind of emotional *Hunger Games,* where I felt like I had to fight tooth and nail to keep the love I thought I deserved. It was an exhausting cycle that left me drained and questioning my worthiness of genuine affection. It was like being stuck in a soap opera that I didn't audition for but couldn't find the exit stage left.

I brought my baggage into every relationship, unpacking my insecurities, fears, and deep-seated feelings of unworthiness. I was perpetuating the cycle of abuse that I had lived through as a child, not physically but emotionally, battering my partners with my pain and confusion.

My relationships were a cry for help, a reflection of the love I longed to receive from my mother. They were my misguided attempts to fill the void her neglect and abuse left. But, as they say, hindsight is 20/20, and it took many trials, errors, and heartaches before I finally started seeing clearly.

There was one relationship, particularly a raw and unedited manuscript of my past. We loved hard, and we fought harder. My anger, a simmering pot always on the verge of boiling over, was ever present, and the slightest disagreement would set off a firework display of fury. Every harsh word thrown was a verbal re-enactment of the hurtful exchanges I had with my mother. Every heated argument felt familiar, a destructive dance I knew too well. My boyfriend became a stand-in for my mother, and I, the rebellious teenager, was continually on the defensive.

And then there was the drama. Oh, the drama. I would create scenarios in my head, each more complicated and tragic than the last, and play them out in reality. I believed, profoundly and erroneously, that love had to be fought for and earned through trials and tribulations. I found a perverse sense of comfort in the chaos's familiarity.

But, you see, there's a certain sadness, an inevitable tragedy in finding solace in chaos. It's like being addicted to the poison, craving something that's killing you slowly. It felt like being trapped in a labyrinth of pain, where every turn leads to more suffering, every path to more heartache. The cycle was relentless, a never-ending loop of pain and reconciliation. Each reconciliation felt like a band-aid, a temporary fix to a festering wound. It was like trying to piece together a shattered mirror, the cracks always visible, the reflections always distorted.

This brew of intense love and pain steeped every fight and makeup session. It felt like walking on a tightrope, where one wrong step, one misjudged word, could plunge you into an abyss of hurt. I became an artisan of pain, molding each argument and confrontation into a work of tragic art. It was like being a puppeteer, pulling the strings, orchestrating the dance of destruction. And in this macabre ballet, love and pain intertwined, creating a tapestry of hurt and passion.

Here's the thing about being steeped in drama—it drains and consumes you. It's like being in a constant state of high alert, waiting for the next crisis, anticipating the next blow. The mind becomes a battlefield, each thought a soldier in a war of emotions. And when you're constantly in the storm's eye, navigating through the upheaval of emotions, you lose yourself. It's like being adrift in a sea of turmoil, where the waves of pain and the winds of anguish threaten to drown you. But, amidst the storm and chaos, there was a flicker of hope, a whisper of a better tomorrow. It was the faint glimmer of the possibility of a love untainted by pain, of a relationship free from the shadows of the past.

To my surprise, that flicker of hope was a jail cell. When the repercussions of my rage landed me in jail, the illusion of the dramatic love story I was living shattered. Imagine me in a cell block with 50 other inmates in a county jail! The echoing slam of the doors was a stark reminder of the harsh reality I found myself in. Each time was a further blow to my self-esteem, a punch to my self-worth. I was reeling, disoriented, caught in the web of the destructive narrative I'd spun for myself.

I wish I could tell you that the first arrest was enough for me to change. But no, it took three stints behind bars and three doses of harsh reality for me to start questioning my path. Each arrest felt like a physical assault, tearing away at my already bruised self-esteem leaving me feeling vulnerable and raw.

Looking back, I see how I replayed the same dysfunctional patterns from childhood, trying to rewrite the story with different characters. I believed, perhaps naively, that if I could make this distorted version of love work, it would somehow validate my experiences and heal the wounds inflicted by my mother.

But love is not a salve you apply to old wounds, hoping they'll miraculously heal. Love is not a reflection of past hurts or a replica of unhealthy patterns. And love should not leave you feeling stripped of your self-worth or sitting in a jail cell questioning your existence. Love isn't supposed to be a battlefield. Love shouldn't inflict pain or demand sacrifices.

Realizing that I was stuck in a cycle of destructive love was like waking up from a bad dream. It was jarring, uncomfortable, and life-altering. But it also marked the beginning of a new chapter in my life. A chapter where I learned that love could be kind, gentle, and supportive. But we're not there yet. Stick with me; there's still a lot of ground to cover.

My work life was entirely another battlefield. Regardless of their actual demeanor or intentions, every boss seemed to morph into a mirror image of my mother. The sound of their voice when they called my name, the way they looked when they were reviewing my work; it was like I was back in my childhood home, bracing myself for the next blow.

Even when constructive, their criticism felt like daggers to my heart, echoing my mother's venomous words. I would internalize their feedback, turning it into self-loathing, convincing myself that I was never good enough, no matter how hard I worked. This paranoia, bred from years of my mother's emotional abuse, bled into my professional life, causing me to over-analyze every interaction, every sideways glance, every casual remark.

Outside of the professional realm, my friendships were also a minefield. My mother's manipulation taught me to second-guess everything, look for hidden motives, and wait for inevitable betrayal. I constantly feared the other shoe dropping - when a friend would reveal their true colors and hurt me, just like my mother used to.

I built walls around myself, convinced it was the only way to prevent further heartache. Even when friends showed genuine care and kindness, I couldn't fully trust them. I'd become so accustomed to emotional manipulation that genuine affection seemed suspicious, a bait leading to a potential trap.

This distrust strained my relationships and made it difficult for me to form meaningful connections. These patterns were exhausting, but they were all I knew. They were survival mechanisms, learned responses from a childhood filled with uncertainty and pain. It took great introspection, therapy, and patience to unravel these patterns.

And family? Our family tree had more than a few branches lopped off, thanks to my mother's antics. My connections were severed individually, leaving me isolated and alone from my grandparents, aunts, uncles, and cousins. My mother had a knack for warping narratives, spinning stories in ways that allowed her to portray herself as the perennial victim. Each interaction, each argument, and each disagreement was expertly manipulated to create a web of misunderstandings and mistrust.

My mother's fallouts always seemed to culminate in me losing access to my family's love and guidance. Phone calls were abruptly disconnected. Visits dwindled until they stopped entirely. Birthday cards, holiday celebrations, all those precious family moments you see framed on walls in sitcom living rooms - they gradually disappeared. My mother was the conductor of this orchestra of disconnection, her baton severing my ties with those who could have been allies, mentors, or simply a loving presence in my life.

But in our twisted family narrative, they, too, were pushed away. Petty disagreements were inflated into irrevocable offenses. Accusations, half-truths, and outright lies were woven into a cloak of isolation that she wrapped around us. Whenever a relative attempted to bridge the gap, I found myself barricaded behind walls my mother had helped me build. Her stories, manipulations, and constant poisoning of my perceptions had turned these family members into enemies in my eyes. They were portrayed as villains in the narratives she wove, and like an unwitting actor, I played my part perfectly. I mirrored her anger, lashing out at these potential allies with fury and resentment.

This was one of the most insidious aspects of my mother's manipulation - she didn't just control my interactions. She manipulated my emotions. She made me her confidante, her ally, her emotional crutch. Yet, simultaneously, she effectively crippled my ability to form authentic, meaningful relationships outside our toxic dyad. My emotional growth was stunted, and my ability to trust others was hampered.

In this emotionally charged environment, isolation was inevitable. Like a tiny island battered by the relentless storm of my mother's emotional chaos, I felt utterly alone. The ties that should have anchored me to a more extensive network of familial love and support were severed until I was adrift. Our family tree, once a symbol of heritage and unity, began to resemble the landscape of our relationship - barren and scarred. The branches that should have burgeoned with nurturing relationships were pruned mercilessly until all that was left was the gnarled trunk, bearing witness to the deep scars of each severed connection.

It was as if we were trapped in a perpetual winter, our family tree stripped bare. And in this desolate landscape, I clung to the only source of connection I knew – my mother, however flawed and damaging that connection was.

This estrangement from family wasn't just a geographical distance but an emotional chasm that yawned wide and deep. It isolated me not just from family but from a part of myself as well. I was cut off from the richness of shared histories, collective memories, and the unconditional love that families can provide.

So, how did I, a young queer kid with a volatile past, navigate this tumultuous sea of emotions and experiences? Music, art, and books were my lifelines, my buoy in the stormy sea of my youth. I've always found an emotional resonance in music - how a melody can wrap around your heart and a lyric can echo your thoughts. It's an art form transcending barriers, a universal language that speaks directly to the soul.

My tastes were eclectic, ranging from empowering rock anthems that made me feel invincible to melancholic pop ballads that seemed to understand my isolation. I'd lock myself in my room, put my headphones on, and lose myself in the rhythm and the rhymes. I wasn't a kid stuck in a toxic environment in those moments. I was a rock star, a poet, and a fearless explorer of sonic landscapes.

Books offered a different escapism. They were my passport to other worlds, realms where I could live vicariously through characters whose lives were far from mine. Heroes and heroines braved their circumstances with courage, villains who were a bit too familiar, and narratives devoid of the manipulations I faced daily. These stories allowed me to imagine different outcomes and dream of a life far beyond reality.

Fantasy novels were a particular favorite of mine because they were as far removed from my real life as possible. There was something comforting about diving into a world where the challenges were clear-cut, and the villains were often defeated.

Eventually, the music stops playing, and the book ends. There comes a point when you have to face reality, and my time came in my mid-thirties. I was physically and mentally burnt out, carrying a lifetime of trauma like a 100-pound backpack. Something had to change.

The narrative of my life took a transformative turn when I crossed paths with the man who would become my husband. He entered my world like a soothing melody, a counterpoint to the cacophony I had become so accustomed to. He was different. His love was different. It was gentle, not gnarled; respectful, not resentful; kind, not cruel.

His very existence was a wake-up call. With every tender word and thoughtful gesture, he painted a picture of a different reality I hadn't allowed myself to imagine before. This was a reality where love wasn't a battlefield, but a sanctuary. Where relationships weren't a tug of war but a mutual support system. Where words weren't used as weapons but as whispers of encouragement. The contrast was stark and startling.

It's funny how certain moments in life can feel like they're straight out of a movie scene. This was one of them, right up there with Simba looking up at Mufasa in the sky scene from *The Lion King*. Instead of a celestial lion imparting wisdom, my husband made dinner in our tiny kitchen, humming along to an old Backstreet Boys tune. And just like that, it hit me: I deserved to be loved, truly and deeply, not in the haphazard, sporadic way that I had known as a child, but with consistency, respect, and gentleness.

This epiphany came with a wave of emotions. There was relief, of course, that I had broken free from my past. But there was also guilt and regret for the relationships I had tainted and the people I had pushed away while I was stuck in those destructive cycles. It was like I had suddenly gained the ability to see the Matrix code and how deeply I had been entangled in it.

I remember feeling a sense of mourning for my younger self, who had been so desperate for love that he had mistaken his mother's abusive behavior for affection. The one who had entered and sustained toxic relationships, thinking that's all he was worthy of. The one who had lived in a constant state of fight-or-flight, unable to envision a life outside of chaos.

But amidst this whirlwind of emotions, there was also an underlying sense of empowerment. I realized that I had been given a second chance to rewrite my narrative, an opportunity that not everyone gets. I now had the power to break the chains of my past and to consciously create a healthier, happier life.

It was like the moment in every superhero movie where the hero finally understands the true extent of their powers. There's always that pivotal scene, you know? Like when Peter Parker first discovers his spidey abilities or when Elsa, in all her icy glory, decides to "let it go" and fully embraces her powers. This was my superhero moment, the turning point where I finally understood I could be my own hero.

From then on, I made a commitment to myself. I would no longer be a prisoner of my past. Instead, I would be an architect of my future, using the bricks of self-love, self-respect, and self-care to build a new foundation for my life.

It was a tough pill to swallow. Recognizing the patterns was one thing, but unlearning them? That was a whole other ball game. It felt like trying to untangle a giant knot of habits, reactions, and emotions I had carried around for the better part of my life.

But I also knew this: If I wanted to share my life with this man - and I did, I really did - I needed to heal for him and me. I owed it to myself to build a healthy, thriving life that was a product of love, not scars. So, I decided. I fought, not with fists, but with faith - faith in myself, in my capacity for change. I decided to learn, not from pain, but from patience - patience with myself, with the process. I healed, not for revenge, but for the redemption of the child within me who deserved so much better.

As I reflect on this tumultuous period of my life, I'm struck by the resilience of the human spirit. It's difficult, painful even, to revisit these dark chapters. Yet, there's an undeniable sense of catharsis in unearthing these past traumas, laying them bare for you to see. I hope that sharing these experiences makes you feel less alone and less shackled by your past.

Understanding the impact of these events was challenging. In fact, it took many years and countless hours in therapy to see the twisted patterns for what they were. But as I navigated through the fog of my past, I found glimmers of clarity and strength. My life had been a chaotic whirlwind, marked by eruptions of anger and deep wells of despair. My mother, who should have been my guiding light, was instead the eye of my storm. She was the source of my deepest pain but also, in a strange twist of fate, my greatest teacher.

But don't get me wrong. This is not a tale of forgiveness, of absolving my mother for the harm she caused. It's a journey of understanding, of breaking the cycle of pain and manipulation. It's about navigating through the storm and coming out on the other side, not unscathed, but stronger.

You might wonder, how did I untangle this mess? How did I rise above the trauma and pain? Well, that's a story for the next chapter. The journey was long and winding, full of potholes and detours. But it led me to where I am today, standing tall, scarred but unbowed, ready to share the lessons I've learned.

As we progress, remember that while the past shapes us, it does not define us. It's part of our story, but only part of the book. The chapters to come are about change, growth, healing, and self-discovery.

So, as we close this chapter, I want you to hold on to one thing:

No matter how twisted the journey and how deep the scars are, it's never too late to heal. It's always possible to turn the page and start a new chapter.

CHAPTER 6

PATHWAYS TO THE SUN: THE PATH TO HEALING

There's no one-size-fits-all solution when it comes to healing from childhood wounds. It's like finding the proper skincare routine - what clears up one person's acne might make another's worse, and what minimizes one person's wrinkles might do nothing for another's. Like in the quest for the perfect complexion, the road to recovery is often fraught with trials and errors, setbacks and breakthroughs, and a lot of patience.

My healing journey began on a therapist's couch but the healing really happened when I put pen to paper. That's right, folks! I decided to go full Ronald Doal and began writing a children's book series. My intention wasn't to make millions or create the next "*James & The Giant Peach*," but rather to reconcile with my inner child, the boy who had been ignored, ridiculed, and belittled, to tell him that he mattered, he was loved, he deserved better.

Think of it like this: I was standing at a fork in the road of my life. One path led me towards the never-ending cycle of anger, frustration, and sadness - a way well-trodden by the tires of my past. The other was overgrown, untamed, a path less traveled, but it offered something the other didn't - hope.

So, I laced up my metaphorical hiking boots, gripped the pen like my walking stick, and took the less traveled road. And that, my friends, has made all the difference.

The process of writing this children's book series was nothing less than transformative. It was like traveling back in time, walking through the playgrounds of my past, seeing my childhood through a different lens. It was no longer the grainy, sepia-toned film I had replayed in my mind for years. Instead, it became a vibrant, technicolor movie, filled with moments of pain and sorrow but also moments of joy, resilience, and courage. It was like watching *The Wizard of Oz* and realizing that I, too, had the power to click my heels and find my way home.

As I penned down the adventures of my characters, I was actually rewriting my own narrative. With every page, every chapter, I was stepping in and standing up for that little boy who needed a champion. I was telling him that his feelings were valid and his experiences accurate. I gave him what he had longed for all those years ago - validation, acceptance, love.

This process of healing through writing, often known as *narrative therapy*, became my safe space, my sanctuary. I could express my thoughts, fears, hopes, and dreams without judgment or fear. The blank pages were my canvas, and I could paint my story how I wanted, not how someone else had dictated. It was empowering, even liberating. And the beautiful thing was, the more I wrote, the more I healed, and the more I recovered, the more I wanted to write. It became a virtuous cycle of self-discovery and self-acceptance. I wasn't just creating a children's book series; I was making a new me, a better me, a healed me.

Remember, there is no "one-size-fits-all" when it comes to healing. Your journey may not start with a pen and paper. It may start with a paintbrush, a musical instrument, a pair of running shoes, or even a quiet moment with a cup of tea. The key is finding what speaks to you, helps you connect with your inner self, and makes you feel heard, seen, and loved. When you find it, embrace it, nurture it, and let it guide you towards your own path to healing.

Professional help like therapy and counseling can also be an excellent choice for many, and I encourage anyone to explore that route if it resonates. Some people find healing through talking with a professional, others through medications, while others might find solace in support groups. You do you. Just like choosing whether to be Team Edward or Team Jacob, it's a highly personal decision.

Whatever path you take, I can't stress this enough - self-care and self-love are not optional extras. They're the heart and soul of the process. They're the Harry to your Hermione, the Rachel to your Monica, and the Spongebob to your Patrick. Self-care is the headliner, not the opening act in the healing world.

Now, when I say 'self-care,' I'm not talking about indulging in any and everything. I'm talking about the deep, sometimes challenging work of honoring and caring for yourself. It's like being your own Beyoncé - independent, fierce, and unapologetically fabulous. And trust me, it's easier said than done.

For me, one of the most significant acts of self-care was learning to sit with my feelings to give them space without immediately reacting. Just like you don't text back instantly when an ex messages you out of the blue, giving your feelings some breathing room is essential. Remember, feelings aren't facts, and just because you feel like you're failing doesn't mean you are any more than eating a Taco Bell Crunchwrap Supreme makes you a Taco Master.

I discovered that sitting with your feelings and giving them space is like allowing each emotion its own reality show episode. Instead of impulsively reacting, I would roll out the metaphorical red carpet, invite the feelings in, and let them have their moment. But like all good reality TV dramas, there were plot twists, shocking turns, and sometimes unexpected endings. It was messy and confusing, but it was also honest and raw.

This practice became a cornerstone of my healing process, and I want to clarify that it's far from easy. When anger shows up, it's like an unwanted house guest that overstays their welcome, and sitting with it can feel as frustrating as trying to untangle a pair of earphones that have been in your pocket for an hour. When sadness comes knocking, it's like being stuck in a downpour without an umbrella, and who really enjoys being soaked to the skin?

But here's the thing - these feelings, as uncomfortable as they might be, matter. Just like each episode of *Friends* contributes to the overall storyline, each feeling and emotion plays a part in the narrative of 'you.'

Acknowledging these feelings, not shoving them aside or burying them under layers of distraction, was one of the most challenging aspects of my healing journey. It requires commitment, patience, and the occasional tub of ice cream for emotional support. It's like inviting uninvited guests to the party of your life; you may not want them there, but the sooner you recognize them, the sooner they might leave. It's natural to want to avoid feelings that cause discomfort or pain, but the longer we ignore them, the more they fester and grow in the background.

Think of it like dealing with a *Sims* game glitch. You can ignore it, sure, but it might lead to your Sim cooking an invisible meal or constantly walking through walls until the entire game crashes. Acknowledging and dealing with the glitch early on is challenging but ultimately much less disruptive. This process isn't an overnight job; it requires a commitment to yourself and a willingness to sit with your feelings, no matter how difficult. It's like choosing to watch a documentary about climate change when you really want to re-watch *Golden Girls* for the tenth time. It differs from what you want to do but is essential and worthwhile.

Patience plays a crucial role, too. Healing takes time. We live in an age of instant gratification, but there are no quick fixes or cheat codes for emotional healing. It's okay to be a "slowpoke" on this journey, taking one step at a time at your own pace. And, of course, it's okay to lean on your version of comfort for emotional support. Whether it's a tub of ice cream, a pint of craft beer, a nostalgic anime binge-watch, or a karaoke night singing Adele's hits at the top of your lungs, give yourself permission to seek comfort and care during this journey. It's perfectly okay to have something that brings comfort and a sense of normalcy when dealing with difficult emotions.

Acknowledging your feelings is the first step towards understanding and managing them. It's a vital part of the healing process, allowing you to rewrite your narrative and take control of your life. Be patient, stay committed, and remember to stock up on your favorite ice cream.

Creating a healthier life narrative meant facing some uncomfortable truths, challenging my harmful beliefs about myself, and gradually rewriting my own story. It required close attention, scrutiny, and a willingness to see things from a new perspective.

I replaced self-deprecation with self-compassion, self-criticism with self-encouragement, and self-neglect with self-care. It was a long process and is still ongoing, but it's worth every moment. Because becoming your own hero is the most empowering journey you can undertake. It takes time, dedication, and a lot of patience, but the sense of accomplishment, growth, and self-love makes it all worthwhile.

Learning to listen to and meet my needs was another pivotal part of my healing journey. It was like making a perfect playlist for myself. Some days, I needed something calming like Sade, and others required the upbeat rhythm of the one and only Britney Spears. Whatever my emotional state, I learned to tune into it and provide for myself what I needed most.

This also meant taking care of my physical health. It's easy to forget about it when you're focused on emotional healing, but your body and mind are like Batman and Robin - they're a team, and one can't work optimally without the other. Regular exercise, balanced nutrition, and adequate rest became as vital to my healing process as therapy and self-reflection. There were days when a good workout felt as cathartic as a heart-to-heart talk and other times when a hearty meal felt as comforting as a warm hug.

Now, I know what you're thinking - this all sounds like a lot of work. And you're right. Healing isn't a walk in the park (unless walking in the garden is part of your healing process). But I want to reassure you that it's okay to take it slowly, one step at a time. It's not a race, and there's no finish line. It's more like binge-watching your favorite series - you can take it at your own pace, and it's okay to pause when it gets too intense.

It's also important to note that setbacks are part of the process. Think of them as plot twists - they're unexpected, they can be upsetting, but they also add depth to the story. When I encountered setbacks, I felt like I had been knocked off my feet, but I learned that it was okay to take some time to recover and to get back up when I was ready.

Remember that episode of *The Fresh Prince of Bel-Air* when Will's father leaves him again, and he breaks down in Uncle Phil's arms? We all felt his pain, his disappointment. But we also saw him rise from it, grow more robust, and move on with his life. That's the kind of resilience we're talking about here.

Each setback and challenge is an opportunity to learn, grow, and strengthen your resilience. It's like leveling up in a video game - you face enemies and encounter obstacles, but you also gain experience, skills, and maybe even some cool power-ups.

Healing is not a linear journey. It's more like playing a game of *Mario Kart*—there are twists, turns, obstacles, and maybe even a few banana peels on the road. But like Mario or Luigi, you're the driver, and you get to decide the pace. Some days, you might race through a course, making progress in leaps and bounds. On other days, you might get hit by a spiky blue shell and need to pause and recollect. What's essential is that you keep going, keep driving forward, even when Rainbow Road feels precarious and unending. Healing isn't about reaching a destination where everything is perfect, and you've got everything figured out. No, recovery is about growth, understanding, and, most importantly, self-love.

So, take a breath, grab a tub of ice cream, and get ready to level up. Because the game of life waits for no one, and trust me, you're more than prepared to play. Keep going, Player One. You've got this. See you in the next chapter.

CHAPTER 7

THE SWITCH: FROM SURVIVING TO LIVING

I should have known that the transition from surviving to living my life wouldn't happen overnight. After all, you don't get out of quicksand by flailing wildly; you do it by taking slow, purposeful steps. Lesbehonest, most of my knowledge about quicksand came from Saturday morning cartoons. But the metaphor still stands!

I'd spent most of my life in fight mode, fists up, braced for the next blow. But after my last stint in jail, I knew something had to change. I couldn't keep being the angry, hurt kid forever.

And so, the switch began.

But the healing process wasn't all rainbows and unicorns like a Lisa Frank binder. There were setbacks. Oh boy, were there setbacks. Remember those crime shows where the detective hits a dead end? Yeah, that was me multiple times. Times when I'd stare at a blank page, the cursor blinking like a taunting adversary. Times when old memories would resurface, so painful that they took my breath away.

But I pressed on.

One of the first things I did was try to understand why I was so angry. The whys were critical. I was like a detective on a crime show, sorting through clues and trying to piece together the puzzle that was my psyche. Therapy helped, sure. I had more therapists on speed dial than I did friends.

Then came the phase of actually dealing with emotions, and let me tell you, that's a whole different beast. Remember Simba's expression when Mufasa tells him about the "great kings of the past"? That was my face when I realized the vast landscape of emotions I'd ignored. But I learned to sit with them, to dissect them like a frog in a high school biology class (minus the gross part). Anger, fear, sadness, they all became less scary when I took the time to understand them.

This journey was about shifting my perspective and habits. I started replacing my old harmful coping mechanisms with positive ones. Instead of binge-watching streaming platforms till my eyes bled when I was feeling down, I'd write, sketch, or take a walk. Each step, each stroke, each word became an act of healing. The transition from surviving to living was like navigating a maze of traps, dead-ends, and a Minotaur or two. But as I stand on the other side of the labyrinth, I can tell you it was worth it. Because life isn't just about surviving; it's about truly living. It's about claiming your narrative, taking control of your journey, and realizing you can switch on the light even on the darkest nights.

I noticed something remarkable as I began to embrace the journey with all its ups and downs. My relationships with others started changing. No longer was I the volatile ticking bomb, ready to explode at any moment. Instead, I found myself becoming more empathetic, more patient, and more understanding. It was like someone had handed me the "cheat codes" to human interactions. I discovered that life was not just about moving from one day to another but about cherishing each moment, each breath. I began to find joy in the small things: the aroma of freshly brewed coffee, the crunch of autumn leaves under my boots, and the feel of my husband's hand in mine.

In essence, it was about changing the narrative, about rewriting the story. And let me tell you, there is a particular power in that. When you stop seeing yourself as a victim and start seeing yourself as the hero of your story, the magic happens.

One of the most enlightening realizations I had during this journey was understanding the power of vulnerability. I spent so much time building walls around myself, armoring up to protect that scared little boy inside. I'd put on a brave face, sporting an Oscar-worthy performance of a guy who had it all together. But in reality, I was a jigsaw puzzle with so many missing pieces, desperately trying to fit into a picture that wasn't mine.

It wasn't until I embraced vulnerability that I felt more "whole." I stopped pretending to be okay when I wasn't. I allowed myself to feel, to hurt, to heal. I learned it was okay to cry, scream, and let out the pent-up emotions I had bottled up for years. It was like releasing the pressure from a shaken soda can. Messy, yes, but also incredibly relieving. And with vulnerability came authenticity. No more masquerades, no more masks. I was no longer playing a character in my life's story; I was living it genuinely and authentically. I began to understand myself better, appreciate my strengths, and accept my flaws. And you know what? That's when I started to like the man I saw in the mirror.

Sure, there were setbacks. I hit a few speed bumps, had a couple of flat tires, and maybe even a breakdown, but with every fall, I rose stronger. I learned to dance in the rain instead of waiting for the storm to pass. Because here's the thing about storms: **they don't last forever**.

One particular challenge that comes to mind was on a random Tuesday. I was sitting in my living room when the weight of the past suddenly came crashing down. It was like every wound, every scar was ripped open again. I was drowning in a sea of pain and sorrow. But instead of fighting it, I let it wash over me. I cried, I screamed, I felt. And when the storm passed, I felt lighter, freer.

Through all the tears and laughter, the breakdowns and breakthroughs, the one thing that remained constant was my determination to heal, grow, and evolve. I emerged stronger and brighter. I began to find beauty in my brokenness and strength in my scars.

I discovered something profound in my journey from surviving to living: I wasn't broken; I was just bent. And with every step I took towards healing, I felt myself straighten a little more. The journey from surviving to living is not just about healing from the past. It's about embracing the future with open arms and an open heart. It's about learning to laugh, to love, to live. And trust me, there's nothing more beautiful than that.

Throughout this chapter, we've journeyed from mere survival into a mindset of fully embracing and living life.

Let's review the essential steps:

1. Recognize and Validate Your Feelings

Recognizing and validating your feelings is not just about telling yourself, "I'm angry" or "I'm sad." It's about allowing yourself to feel these emotions without judgment, guilt, or needing to immediately "fix" them. It's about understanding that these emotions are reactions to your experiences and reflections of your human resilience.

Imagine a scene from a '90s sitcom (you know, for the nostalgia). A character feels blue, so they wrap themselves in a blanket, put on a sad movie, and let the tears flow while eating a pint of ice cream straight from the carton. It's comedic, sure, but there's something therapeutic in it. Giving yourself the space to feel, cry, be angry, and grieve is all part of the healing process.

Journaling is an excellent tool for validating your feelings. It's like conversing with yourself, a safe space where you can be honest about your emotions. And remember, this journal is for your eyes only. Feel free to be as raw and uncensored as you need to be.

If you're more of a talker than a writer, consider speaking with a close friend or a loved one. Let them know you don't need solutions or advice—you need to be heard. And if you can't find that person, that's okay. A therapist can be that impartial, non-judgmental ear. It's like having a living, breathing Google search, ready with strategies and exercises to help you navigate your emotional landscape. And I promise, they won't judge you like your search history probably does.

In short, recognizing and validating your feelings can be likened to turning on your favorite tear-jerker movie and giving yourself permission to cry. Let it out, let it flow. Because only when we acknowledge our pain can we begin the journey of healing it. And who knows? You may eventually have a 'Life is like a box of chocolates' revelation and find the strength you never knew you had. Now, pass the popcorn.

2.   Adopt a Living Mindset

Shifting from existing to living is like waking up from hibernation - a long winter of discontent, you could say - and stepping into the sunshine of spring. In the same way, a bear groggily shakes off sleep and looks for that first delicious mouthful of fresh salmon. Making the shift requires you to shake off old habits and reach for new, nourishing experiences.

It's like when Belle from *Beauty and the Beast* decides she wants "adventure in the great wide somewhere." It's about wanting more than your provincial life, stepping out of your comfort zone, and embracing the unknown.

This mindset shift involved a conscious decision to not let my past dictate my present or future. It's like I was Harry Potter; my past was a Horcrux I had to destroy. Remember how each Horcrux took a part of Harry's soul? That's what my past was doing to me. I had to find and destroy my Horcruxes to reclaim my soul and live fully. But how do you do that? It begins with mindful awareness. This is about tuning into your thoughts, feelings, and behaviors and recognizing when they're being influenced by past traumas.

The next step is to develop coping strategies to keep the "demons" at bay. For some, it could be therapy or counseling. For others, it could be journaling, meditation, working out, or yoga. Find what works for you and stick with it.

Finally, embrace the present moment and the possibilities it brings. Start envisioning a future where you're not just surviving but thriving. This isn't about forgetting the past but learning from it and using it as a stepping stone towards a better future. So go ahead, be the Belle of your life, destroy those Horcruxes, and keep the "demons" at bay. It's your time to live, not just exist. Because, in the words of Dr. Seuss, "*Today you are You, that is truer than true. There is no one alive who is Youer than You.*"

3. Embrace Vulnerability

When I say "embrace vulnerability,"' I know it might sound
as terrifying as answering a phone call when you don't
recognize the number (seriously, who does that?). We often
associate vulnerability with fear, danger, and the risk of
getting hurt. But in reality, vulnerability is less about the
monsters lurking under your bed and more about the
monster inside your closet. And by monster, I mean that
dusty box of feelings you've been too afraid to unpack.

Embracing vulnerability means opening that box. It
means confronting the emotions you've kept hidden, the
memories that still sting, and the self-doubts that echo in
your mind. It's like facing the Mirror of Erised from *Harry
Potter*, and instead of seeing what you desire most, you're
acknowledging your deepest fears, wounds, and regrets.
For example, a big part of my healing journey involved
admitting that my mother's behavior wasn't just 'quirky' or
'strict'—it was abusive. I had to accept that her gaslighting
was not a form of love but a manipulative tactic. I had to
face that I had spent much of my life yearning for her
approval, even at the cost of my happiness. Admitting this
to myself, let alone to my husband and my friends, felt like
standing naked in a room full of people. It was terrifying,
yes, but also liberating.

When you open yourself up this way, you allow
yourself to feel hurt, grief, and rage. You also give yourself
the chance to heal, grow, and learn. Being vulnerable allows
you to release the pain holding you back and make room for
new emotions, experiences, and relationships. It's like doing
a software update for your emotional system. And I won't lie
to you—waiting for your iPhone to install the latest iOS can

be annoying and time-consuming. But the result, like enjoying new emojis and a glitch-free interface, is worth it. You come out stronger, healthier, and more resilient.

By embracing vulnerability, you're not showing weakness but immense strength. You're choosing to confront the wounds of your past head-on, even when it's painful. It's like pulling a band-aid off an injury—you can either rip it off quickly or slowly peel it back, but either way, it's gotta come off for the wound to heal.

So, don't fear vulnerability. Embrace it; it is your ticket to healing, growth, and a better, brighter future. After all, you know what they say about what happens when one door closes. But in this case, you're not waiting for another to open—you're grabbing the doorknob of vulnerability and swinging it wide open yourself.

4. Be Authentic

When I say "be authentic," I don't just mean sharing your favorite Netflix binge or that you prefer thin crust pizza over deep dish (though those are parts of you, too!). I'm talking about peeling back the layers of self-defense and societal conditioning to reveal your innermost fears, desires, dreams, and scars. I'm talking about baring your soul, even when it's terrifying. It's about learning to say, "This is me. I am enough. I am worthy."

Imagine you've spent your whole life in a birdcage, confined and restrained. You've internalized the bars as part of your reality to the point where you can't see beyond them. Authenticity is like finding the courage to open that cage door, to spread your wings, and to explore the vastness of the sky beyond. For instance, think about the hilarious and equally cringey conversations that take place in *The Office*. The characters are raw, honest, and often uncomfortably authentic. They say things we'd only think about in our heads. Embodying this level of authenticity can feel scary, even foolish, at first, but it's liberating in a way words can't fully capture.

In my case, I spent years trying to fit into the mold of whom I thought I should be - the dutiful son, the peacemaker, the person who held it all together, even when everything was falling apart. I tried to make myself smaller, quieter, and less noticeable. And you know what? It was exhausting. Like trying to hold my breath underwater while pretending I was chilling in a hot tub.

When I started being authentic—being true to my feelings, identity, and experiences— I began to breathe freely. I realized that I wasn't the bad kid my mother painted me to be. I wasn't the unruly child, the troublemaker, or the liar. I was a person who had been hurt, who had suffered. And acknowledging that was an essential part of my journey toward healing and self-love. Authenticity involves being honest about your past and acknowledging its impact on your life. This isn't about placing blame or wallowing in self-pity; it's about understanding and controlling your narrative. Like Oprah says, "You are not your circumstances. You are your possibilities."

Here's your homework: Start being true to yourself. Embrace your quirks, your flaws, your passions, and your dreams. Open that cage door, spread your wings, and fly. You might just be surprised at how liberating authenticity can feel.

5. Find Strength in Your Scars

When I started on this healing journey, I saw my scars, both symbolic and real, as symbols of my painful past. They were ugly reminders of a childhood marred by trauma, tokens of a past I desperately wanted to forget. But over time, my perspective started to shift. I began to see these scars not as signs of victimhood but as badges of survival. It's like Harry Potter's lightning bolt scar—a mark of an attempt to destroy him, yet he survived. In reality, it's a bit more grim, but you get the idea.

Think of it this way. You know how millennials love their avocado toasts, right? Imagine life as a piece of that perfectly toasted, crusty sourdough bread. The traumas, hurtful incidents, and abuses are like the deep pits in the avocado slices. But here's the thing. Just because the avocado has pits doesn't mean it can't be a part of a delicious meal. The same goes for your life. The scars and pits of your past don't define your worth, but they contribute to your unique flavor. Each scar tells a story. A story of survival, resilience, and strength. They're a testament to the storms you've weathered and the battles you've won. They're symbols of your capacity to heal, grow, and transform. In Japan, there's an art form known as Kintsugi, where broken pottery is repaired with gold, making the cracks a part of the piece's beauty. The philosophy behind it is that breakage and repair are part of the history of an object and should not be hidden. Your scars are your gold lines, your marks of resilience.

Moreover, these scars can become a source of empowerment. They show that you've faced the darkest corners of life and came out stronger on the other side.

They remind you of your resilience and courage, whispering that if you can survive, you can survive anything. By embracing your scars, you reclaim your narrative. You turn your history of pain into a future of possibilities. Just like the vibrant phoenix rises from the ashes, you too can rise from your past, not in spite of your scars, but because of them. You are the living, breathing proof of the saying, "*What doesn't kill you makes you stronger.*" And believe me, you are stronger than you realize. So rock your scars like a boss, and let them testify to your strength.

6. Dance in the Rain

Dancing in the rain may sound like a metaphor from some angst-filled teenage drama movie or a cliché Instagram caption. Still, it holds an essential truth: finding joy, peace, and meaning amid adversity is fundamental to healing. For me, "dancing in the rain" wasn't about disregarding the storm around me, pretending my past didn't exist or that my traumas were suddenly unimportant. No, it was more like embracing the reality of the storm, accepting its presence, but refusing to let it wash away my resilience and spirit.

I'm reminded of a time during my senior year of high school. Remember when the iPod came out, and it was all the rage? I had saved enough from my part-time job to buy one and cherished that tiny device like a precious gem.

One afternoon, after a particularly rough encounter with my mother, I found solace in my music. I remember sitting in my room, tears streaming down my face, the new Jewel album blaring in my ears. But even in that moment of pain, I found myself tapping my foot, lost in Jewels' impeccable voice and relatable lyrics. That was my version of dancing in the rain.

It was the same when I started to unravel the tangled mess of my childhood and confront my traumas. There were dark days, believe me, days filled with anger, regret, and sadness. Yet, amidst that emotional upheaval, I discovered pockets of peace in unexpected places.

I found solace in writing. As a kid, I always enjoyed creating stories, so I returned to that old hobby. Writing became my refuge, a safe space to explore my emotions and experiences without judgment. I wrote about my experiences, imaginary worlds, and the kind of love I wished I had received as a child.

My husband was an unwavering pillar of support throughout this journey. His patience, understanding, and ridiculous jokes were a constant source of comfort.

I found joy in little things like a perfect cup of coffee in the morning, the infectious laughter of my nieces and nephews, the satisfaction of completing a challenging puzzle, or the exhilarating freedom of singing my lungs out at a concert (Sorry, not sorry, Mariah Carey. Those high notes are irresistible!).

When you're caught in a storm, it's easy to focus only on the thunder, the lightning, and the torrential downpour. But once you start looking for opportunities to dance, to find joy and peace, you'll be surprised at how many you find. And slowly but surely, you'll learn to dance even in the hardest rain, knowing that you're surviving and living.

And so, I leave you with this thought as we close this chapter: If I can rewrite my narrative, **so can you**. If I, a kid who once thought love was measured in shouting matches and fists, can find true love and happiness, **so can you**. If I can switch from surviving to living, **so can you**.

Remember, no matter how the story started, you hold the pen. You have the power to write your own ending.

CHAPTER 8

BLUEPRINTS FOR BRIDGES: CREATING HEALTHY RELATIONSHIPS

Let's be real. Relationships are a bit like assembling IKEA furniture. They come with instructions that often look like gibberish, parts you can't find a purpose for, and the inevitable realization that you're using the wrong screwdriver for the job. But, like that strangely named IKEA bookshelf, if you manage to put it together right, you'll get something great out of it. Or, at least, somewhere to put your Funko Pops.

QUESTIONS

What are some ways in which you've allowed people to cross your boundaries in the past?

How did it make you feel?

BUILDING BLOCKS OF BOUNDARIES

Boundary setting is a bit like putting up your personal 'Beware of the Dog' sign – except you're not a dog; you're a human with feelings and anyone who can't respect that? Well, they can play fetch elsewhere.

The Importance of Setting Boundaries

Let's discuss setting boundaries, the interpersonal version of the 'No Trespassing' sign. It's about understanding and communicating your needs, limits, and expectations in a relationship. It's like explaining to your friends that, no, they cannot spoil the latest movie for you, and yes, they will face your wrath if they try.

TIP: *When setting boundaries, remember to assert them clearly and stand by them, even when others push back.*

REFLECTIVE
QUESTIONS

Can you recall a time when you stood firm on your boundaries?

What was the outcome?

Just as a house has walls and fences to keep unwanted visitors out, so should you have personal boundaries to safeguard your emotional and mental well-being. Now, if only these boundaries came with a complimentary moat and a castle tower! But, our weapons in the modern world are clear communication and assertiveness.

Here's the expanded scoop on setting boundaries:

The Steps to Setting Boundaries

1. **Identify Your Limits: Know your comfort zones in various aspects—personal space, time spent, etc.**

   To set a boundary, first, identify your personal limits. Ever felt like you're living in a perpetual "Mean Girls" day, and you've just been personally victimized by Regina George one too many times? That's your limit. In any relationship, it could be anything—how much time you spend together, how you're spoken to, your personal space, or your right to silence your phone and lose yourself in a good book or show.

2. **Communicate Them: Make your boundaries known explicitly.**

   Once you've identified your limits, it's crucial to communicate them. Unfortunately, we're not all as intuitive as Cady Heron in math class. So be as clear as the Burn Book: say, "*I need some alone* time," or "*I'd appreciate it if you didn't raise your voice when discussing something.*"

3. **Be Assertive but Respectful: There's no need for aggressive behavior when stating what you need.**

This is one that I really struggled with. Assertiveness isn't about being aggressive or bulldozing over others' feelings. It's about expressing your needs and standing up for yourself respectfully and fairly. It's like politely, yet firmly, telling your co-workers that they can't keep stealing your lunch from the office fridge - even if it looks delicious.

Being assertive also means saying 'NO' when you need to. Remember, you can't pour from an empty cup. You need to take care of your needs before you can be there for others.

Be direct and explicit. It's crucial to use an assertive yet respectful tone when setting boundaries. You aren't Darth Vader force-choking your subordinates; you're just a person asking for respect and understanding.

For years, my boundaries were non-existent. My mother bulldozed through them as if they were nothing more than whispers. I realized I had to change this pattern. It wasn't a cakewalk. I had moments where I had to go full-on Regina George, declaring, 'You can't sit with us!' when people tried to trample over my freshly drawn boundaries. I learned to stand my ground, utilizing assertive communication without backing down. Remember, it's okay if people react negatively to your boundaries. That doesn't mean your boundaries are wrong or should be abandoned. Instead, it's a reflection of them, not you. It's crucial to stand by your boundaries, even when others push back.

Your boundaries are your personal shield, keeping you safe and healthy. They're your superpower in maintaining respectful and nurturing relationships. So use them wisely, and don't let anyone else try to shrink them.

Regarding assertiveness, think of it less as being a bull in a china shop and more like being the shepherd tending to your own personal flock. Assertiveness is not about charging through life, throwing your weight around, or taking what you want at the expense of others. It's about managing your space and guiding your interactions with others respectfully and confidently.

Think of your personal boundaries as a circle around you, like an invisible superhero force field. This shield is flexible and can change based on your needs and circumstances. But it's there to protect you, to keep out what doesn't serve you and let in what does. Assertiveness is your power to maintain this shield; it comes in handy when you least expect it.

Imagine this scenario: You're at work, and your colleague, who's like a human black hole for food, has a habit of raiding the office fridge and scarfing down your lovingly prepared Tupperware delicacies. Instead of getting angry or passive-aggressive, an assertive approach would be to approach your colleague and calmly yet firmly address the issue.

You could say, "*Hey, I noticed you've been enjoying my meals lately. I understand we all forget lunch sometimes, but I take the time to prepare these meals for myself. In the future, I'd appreciate it if you could bring your own lunch or ask before taking someone else's. Thanks.*"

See what we did there? We acknowledged the issue, expressed our needs, and offered a solution—all without throwing a punch or nasty comments. This is the power of assertiveness.

EXCERCISE:

Practice saying 'NO' in a mirror.

Feel the empowerment that comes from setting your own boundaries. I know you're rolling your eyes while reading this, but trust me.

Let's not stop there. Assertiveness isn't just about communicating with others—it's also about listening to yourself and standing up for your needs, even if that means saying no. Saying 'NO' can sometimes feel like swallowing a pineapple whole, primarily if you're used to pleasing others. But remember, each time you say 'YES' to something you really don't want, you're saying 'NO' to yourself.

Think of 'NO' as your pause button, a tool that allows you to stop, reassess, and make decisions that align with your needs and values. Initially, it may feel as challenging as understanding a TikTok dance trend on the first try, but with practice, it gets easier. Mastering the art of assertiveness is like learning to salsa dance. It may feel awkward initially, and you might step on a few toes. But with time, you'll find your rhythm, and before you know it, you'll be twirling through life with confidence, grace, and a Tupperware full of untouched deliciousness.

Constructing Your Blueprint

Just like those IKEA instructions, creating and maintaining healthy relationships requires a clear blueprint. It's about determining what you want and need from the relationship and what you can give in return. It's a give and take, a balancing act that requires attention and care. So, how do we create this relationship blueprint?

1) **Identify Your Needs: Understand What You Need from the Relationship**

Start by identifying what you need from the relationship. Do you need support, understanding, love, trust, space, communication, or respect? Do you need a listening ear, a shoulder to lean on, a cheerleader in your corner, or someone who respects your need for space? From there, build on these needs, identify the boundaries that protect them, and practice assertiveness to communicate them.

Constructing a relationship blueprint is a bit like creating your personal recipe for the perfect friendship or partnership or a bit like figuring out how to put together that fucking bookshelf. The instructions might be unclear, but when you take the time to decipher them, you'll know exactly how to assemble a sturdy, well-built relationship that can withstand any weight.

First, it's about determining what you want and need from your relationships. And remember, we're not just talking about romantic partners here – this applies to friendships, work relationships, and even family ties.

I craved understanding and acceptance, something my mother never gave me. I needed someone who would genuinely listen without judgment or immediate advice. I needed someone who would respect my boundaries, quirks, and love for cheesy '90s pop music (*N SYNC forever, am I right?).

2) Recognize Your Offerings: Know What You Bring to the Table

Understanding what you offer is as important as knowing what you want to receive. Are you a great listener? Do you offer sage advice, emotional support, or light-hearted humor? Recognizing your strengths helps you understand the balance of giving and receiving in your relationships.

EXCERCISE:

Make a list of attributes or qualities that you believe you bring into your relationships. How do these contribute to the overall health of the relationship?

3) Establish Boundaries: Protect Your Needs with Well-Defined Limits

Once you know your needs and offerings, you can create boundaries to protect those needs. For instance, if one of your needs is to have alone time to recharge, a boundary might be that you need an hour alone each day. Make sure to establish these limits clearly for yourself and the people around you.

TIP:

Boundaries aren't just about saying 'no'; they can also be about saying 'yes' to things that nourish you. For example, saying 'yes' to spending quality time with loved ones.

4) Apply Assertiveness: Use it to Communicate Your Boundaries

Assertiveness is the method by which you construct and maintain the blueprint. It is the communication tool you use to ensure your boundaries are respected, and your needs are met. Being assertive isn't about being confrontational; it's about expressing yourself clearly, directly, and respectfully. It means standing your ground while respecting the boundaries of others.

By paying close attention to these four components, you create a relationship blueprint that serves you and the other people in your life.

And remember, this blueprint isn't set in stone. Like any good architect, you'll make revisions as you go, adapting the structure to better suit your evolving needs and those of your relationships.

EXCERCISE:

Role-play a scenario where you would need to be assertive in expressing a boundary. How did you feel before, during, and after the exercise?

REFLECTIVE
QUESTION

Now that you have a clearer understanding of the elements in your blueprint, which relationships in your life could benefit from this newfound clarity?

BLUEPRINT

Identify Your Needs: "What You Need from the Relationship"

Understanding: I need a partner who understands my moods and feelings, one who listens without jumping to conclusions.

Space: I value my personal time and space; I need someone who respects that.

Communication: Open, honest conversations are essential.

Trust: Implicit trust is a cornerstone; I can't worry about deception or hidden agendas.

Affection: I need a balanced amount of physical and emotional affection.

Recognize Your Offerings: "What You Bring to the Table"

Emotional Support: I can be that rock, a safe haven during storms.

Humor: I bring levity and laughter to lighten the burdens of life.

Financial Stability: I'm a steady earner and good at budgeting.

Adventure: I enjoy exploring new things and will be an enthusiastic partner in adventures.

Love and Care: I offer a caring, loving space for my partner.

Establish Boundaries: "Well-Defined Limits to Protect Your Needs"

Personal Time: I need at least an hour of 'me' time every day.

Trust and Privacy: No peeking into my personal messages unless explicitly given permission.

Decision-making: Both partners have an equal say in major life decisions.

Conflict Resolution: No name-calling or hitting below the belt during arguments.

Social Interactions: I won't tolerate being belittled or embarrassed in public.

Apply Assertiveness: "Communicating Your Boundaries Clearly"

Personal Time: "I need an hour alone each day to unwind. It's important for my mental health."

Trust and Privacy: "I value my privacy, and I trust you. I expect the same in return."

Decision-making: "Let's make sure we both agree on major decisions that affect us."

Conflict Resolution: "If we argue, let's keep it clean—no name-calling or low blows."

Social Interactions: "Please respect me, especially when we're in public settings."

This blueprint can be modified to suit individual relationships and is by no means a one-size-fits-all. It's a living document that evolves with you and your relationship needs. Remember, setting boundaries isn't just about protecting yourself; it's also about fostering a respectful and loving relationship where both parties feel valued and cared for.

Putting it all together, your relationship blueprint becomes a map to healthier, happier connections. It takes time to draft, and you'll likely make revisions along the way. However, having this blueprint can empower you to seek the relationships you deserve and to break away from the patterns of the past.

So, dear reader, let's queue that playlist, grab some snacks, mark our no-go zones, and start this road trip to Relationshipville. Seatbelts on, let's go!

EXCERCISE:

Draft a relationship blueprint. Start with your needs, then your offerings, and finally list the boundaries that protect those needs.

CHAPTER 9

SELF-SUFFICIENCY: FINDING HAPPINESS WITHIN YOURSELF

If there's one thing that I want you to remember from my story, it's that you're the hero of your own narrative, the captain of your ship, and the star of your show. But being a star isn't just about the glitz and glamour; it's also about the grit, the resilience, and the quiet strength you cultivate within. This is what it means to be self-sufficient. Self-sufficiency often evokes images of adulting—doing taxes, cooking meals, or fixing a leaky faucet. But here, we're not talking about autonomy; we're talking about emotional independence. It's about finding happiness within yourself rather than seeking it in others.

THE POWER OR EMOTIONAL SELF-SUFFICIENCY

Now, don't get me wrong. Human beings are social creatures. We thrive on connection and belonging. We need each other. But as my traumatic experiences taught me, sometimes the people we rely on the most can disappoint us. Sometimes, they can inflict the deepest wounds.

This is why knowing how to stand alone is crucial to finding happiness and fulfillment within yourself. Because at the end of the day, the one person who will always be there for you, no matter what, is YOU. Being emotionally self-sufficient doesn't mean you don't need others; it just means you know how to pick yourself up, dust yourself off, and keep going, even when others let you down.

Emotional self-sufficiency is like having a well inside of you. It's a source of strength, resilience, and happiness you can tap into whenever necessary. It's about knowing that you can cope with whatever life throws at you and that your joy doesn't have to depend on other people or external circumstances.

Building Inner Resilience

One of the critical aspects of emotional self-sufficiency is building inner resilience, which can be seen as your internal 'bounce-back' muscle. Imagine strength as a dynamic shock absorber, cushioning the impact of life's blows and helping you rebound, ready to continue your journey.

1. Understanding Resilience

It's essential to understand what resilience is and what it isn't. Resilience doesn't mean avoiding or ignoring pain, disappointment, or difficulty. Life will have challenging moments, and it's natural to feel upset, anxious, or discouraged at times. What resilience does mean is being able to confront these feelings, endure them, and eventually bounce back.

Think of resilience as that iconic Nokia phone. It could be thrown against a wall, dropped from a two-story building, and even run over by a car, yet it kept working. It was battered and bruised, but it could still do what it was made to do - connect people. And, oh boy, how it rocked at playing Snake. But I digress...The concept of resilience isn't far from that. You are the Nokia in this metaphor. Life might throw you against a wall or drop you from great heights - metaphorically speaking. Your casing might get scratched, and your screen might crack a bit. But guess what? You're still here, aren't you? You can still love, grow, and live a meaningful life. The key is acknowledging the scratches and cracks and not letting them define you.

Resilience is not about being impervious to pain or hardship. Trust me, I wish it were. Life would be so much easier. But we are not Teflon-coated; we're not designed to let things slide off us without leaving a mark. Instead, resilience is about acknowledging the pain, the hardship, the injustice - feeling the total weight of it - and then saying, *"Okay, what's next?"* It's about learning from our experiences, growing stronger, and moving forward. Resilience is not the absence of vulnerability, either. In the words of the great Brené Brown, *"Vulnerability is not winning or losing; it's having the courage to show up and be seen when we have no control over the outcome."* Embracing our vulnerability and allowing ourselves to feel and hurt is part of the journey to resilience.

Remember the '90s cartoon, *Hey Arnold?* Arnold lived in a dysfunctional boarding house, dealt with various trials and tribulations in his urban neighborhood, and let's not forget his struggles with unrequited love (I'm looking at you, Helga). Despite his challenging surroundings, Arnold consistently demonstrated a level-headed, empathetic, and optimistic spirit. He is a perfect example of resilience.

Finally, resilience is about the courage to ask for help when needed. Don't hesitate to seek support from others - be it friends, family, or professionals. We are social creatures, and together we are stronger. Building resilience is a journey, not a destination. It's like going on a road trip without a map but with an endless playlist of your favorite songs. It's tough, it's unpredictable, but with every mile, you're becoming a better driver, learning how to handle the bumps and curves the road throws at you.

2. Cultivating a Positive Outlook

Cultivating a positive outlook is one of the key ways to build resilience. Optimism can empower you to seek solutions rather than dwelling on the problem. This isn't about ignoring reality or sugar-coating challenges but focusing on possibilities and progress. Even in the darkest times, there is always some sliver of light, and it's your job to find and hold onto it. Cultivating this outlook can be challenging, especially when you've been raised in an environment where negativity and criticism are the norm. But think of it as you would care for a plant - it starts with a seed, some fertile soil, a splash of water, and a ray of sunshine. That seed of positivity is already within you, waiting to sprout and grow.

Initially, my seed of positivity was like a cactus - a tiny, prickly ball barely visible in the vast desert of my despair. It was something tough and resilient to survive even in the harshest conditions, and I held onto it dearly. But with time, attention, and care, it started to flourish. I went from a pessimistic tumbleweed, blown around by the whims of my circumstances, to a Joshua tree rooted firmly in my resilience.

At first, it might feel like you're lying to yourself. How can you be positive when you're hurt and angry, right? It feels as fake as a reality TV show. But remember, it's not about denying your feelings or pretending everything is fine when it's not. It's about seeing the good in yourself and the world, even when it is difficult.

Think of positivity as a high-quality Instagram filter for your life. Not the kind that alters your facial features to the point of being unrecognizable, but the one that enhances the colors already present, brightens the light and gently blurs out the unnecessary background noise. Just like mastering the art of the perfect filter, cultivating positivity gets easier with practice. Start with the small things: savor the rich aroma of a good cup of coffee or bask in the warmth of the sun. Gradually, you can shift this appreciation to bigger aspects of your life: recognizing your strengths, celebrating your achievements, and cherishing the love and support surrounding you.

It's also helpful to develop a positive mantra or affirmation. Mine was: "*I am not defined by my past, but I am empowered by it.*" Whenever I felt overwhelmed by negativity, I repeated this mantra, like a catchy pop song chorus that gets stuck in your head, and it helped shift my perspective.

Cultivating a positive outlook is not an overnight transformation; it's a continuous journey. But by shifting your focus from dwelling on problems to seeking solutions and celebrating progress, you can significantly enhance your resilience and overall well-being. Like a moth to a flame, your life will gravitate towards the light you choose to ignite and nurture within yourself.

3. Embracing Change

Part of building resilience is being comfortable with change and even expecting it. Change is a part of life, and adapting is a crucial resilience skill. Remember that change doesn't automatically mean something negative. Many times, change can lead to growth and new opportunities.

Imagine this: you're playing *Super Mario Bros* and memorized every detail of the first level. You've mastered the timing of the jumps, you know precisely where that hidden power-up mushroom is, and you've figured out how to trick the Goombas into walking off the edge. You're comfortable. It's easy. But staying in that first level forever doesn't let you progress. You don't get to save Princess Peach or experience the thrill of navigating the entire Mushroom Kingdom.

Change in life is like moving to the next level in a game. It's unfamiliar, sure, and might even be a little scary. But it's also where the real adventure begins. It's where you grow, learn new skills, and discover your strengths. In fact, I'd argue that it's only through facing the fire-spitting piranha plants and dodging the pesky Boos that Mario really becomes Super Mario.

And isn't that what we want in our lives? To level up, face new challenges, and realize our full potential?

Like in our beloved video game, change in our lives is inevitable. The scenery will change, the challenges will differ, and yes, we might lose a life or two. But each change also brings with it an opportunity to grow, to learn, and to adapt. And let me tell you, no power-up mushroom can replace the feeling of accomplishment when you navigate these challenges yourself.

When I first began my healing journey, the change was scary. But with every step, I was learning more about myself, my resilience, and my ability to adapt. The difference, though intimidating, was liberating. So, let's embrace change, even when it scares us. Let's be open to the opportunities and growth it can inspire. Whether it's ending a toxic relationship, starting therapy, or simply acknowledging your past and seeking healing, remember - you are not losing a level. You're just moving on to the next one. And who knows? You might find a 1-Up Mushroom along the way.

4. Developing a Strong Support Network

While resilience is an internal process, it's not a solitary one. A strong support network consisting of family, friends, or mentors can play a crucial role in helping you cultivate resilience. They can provide perspective, advice, and a listening ear when times are tough.

Think of your support network as your personal *Avengers* team—each member brings unique powers to the table, and together, they help you take on the world. In my case, my support network was more like the cast of *Friends* - minus the unrealistic New York apartment, but with all the warm, fuzzy camaraderie and witty one-liners. For instance, my husband is my own Monica Geller—organized, understanding, and the ultimate caregiver. He's the one who brought stability and a loving presence into my life. He reminded me it's okay to lean on others and that love shouldn't involve fear or manipulation. When I felt lost, he was the lighthouse guiding me back to safety, reminding me that not all was gloom and doom.

Then there are friends - your Phoebe Buffays and Joey Tribbianis. They're your confidants, your partners in crime, who can make you laugh until your stomach hurts and you're gasping for air. They show up at your door at midnight with a tub of ice cream when you're feeling low, and they're the first ones to cheer you on when you score a victory, no matter how small. They remind you that, as dark as things might get, there's always room for laughter, a lot of ice cream, and endless reruns of the *Golden Girls*.

Next up, mentors. They're the Ross Gellers of the group (hopefully minus the three divorces), offering wisdom, advice, and sometimes, tough love. Whether it's a boss, a teacher, or an old family friend, these are the folks who've been around the block. They've weathered their own storms and emerged stronger. They're the ones who can help you see the bigger picture when you're lost in the details. They've got the life experience and the perspective to guide you through the labyrinth of life.

Building this support network is not about finding people who will solve your problems for you. Instead, it's about surrounding yourself with individuals who will stand by you as you solve them. They won't take over the steering wheel, but they'll be there, riding shotgun, cheering you on, and occasionally grabbing the map when you're going in circles. Remember, you don't have to go through this journey alone. My support network has been my lifeline as I've navigated my way from surviving to thriving. They've shared in my pain, victories, breakdowns, and breakthroughs. They've been there for the tears, the laughter, and everything. And let me tell you, it's made all the difference.

So take a leaf out of the *Friends* theme song—find the ones who'll be there for you when the rain starts to pour. Because this journey, while tough, becomes much more manageable when you have your personal *Avengers*, or *Friends* squad by your side.

5. Practicing Self-Care

Regular self-care is an integral part of building resilience. This means taking care of your physical health through regular exercise, a balanced diet, and enough sleep. It also means taking care of your mental and emotional health, such as practicing mindfulness, pursuing hobbies, or simply taking time out for relaxation.

Self-care is not just about bubble baths and face masks (though, don't get me wrong, those are fabulous, too). It's about recognizing that your needs matter and that putting yourself first is not only okay but crucial. It's like when you're on an airplane, and they tell you to secure your oxygen mask before helping others. You can't serve cocktails from an empty shaker.

Let's start with physical self-care. You've heard it a million times. Eat your vegetables, exercise, and get plenty of sleep. And you might be thinking, "Yeah, yeah, I've heard it all before". But trust me, this advice is repeated so often for a reason. A healthy body healthy mind is not just a catchy slogan. Regular exercise doesn't just make you look like Chris Hemsworth in *Thor*. It releases endorphins, those feel-good hormones that improve your mood and act as natural painkillers.

Eating a balanced diet is another part of this equation. I'm not saying you must go full Gwyneth Paltrow and subsist on kale smoothies and gluten-free air. But ensuring you're nourishing your body with plenty of fruits, vegetables, and lean proteins can help regulate your mood, improve your energy levels, and keep you feeling your best. And remember hydration! A lack of water is like a Twitter feed without drama—it just doesn't function right.

Getting enough sleep is another non-negotiable part of self-care. You wouldn't run your car on empty, so why do it to your body? Those late-night Netflix binges seem like a good idea, but adequate sleep is crucial for maintaining mental and physical health. It improves your concentration, regulates mood, and keeps your immune system fighting.

Now, let's talk about mental and emotional self-care. This can be anything from journaling and meditation to belting out Britney's hits in the shower (my favorite). The point is to carve out time to do something that brings you joy, calm, or a sense of satisfaction. Mindfulness, for instance, can be a great tool. Think of it as being the DJ Khaled of your life, constantly reminding yourself, "Hey, I'm here, this is now." It's about focusing on the present moment without judgment. This could be through meditation, yoga, or simply taking a few minutes each day to focus on your breathing.

Lastly, remember to take time for relaxation. Whether reading a good book, binge-watching *Sex & The City* for the third time, or cuddling with your pet, it's essential to give yourself permission to rest and recharge.

At the end of the day, self-care is all about treating yourself with the kindness, patience, and understanding you deserve. It's about reminding yourself that you are worthy of care and love from others and from yourself. It's about turning off your '90s dial-up internet connection and upgrading to the high-speed, all-you-can-handle love and care you deserve. Because in this story, you are the main character, the hero, and it's time to treat yourself like one.

6. Embracing Failure as a Learning Opportunity

Resilience is also about how you view failure. Instead of seeing failure as a negative endpoint, resilient individuals see it as a learning opportunity. Each failure brings valuable lessons that can guide future actions and decisions.

Just like everyone else, I've had my fair share of failures. Times when I made mistakes, messed up, or just outright failed. And let me tell you, in those moments, I felt like Ross on his third divorce— desperate to make people see past my failures and emphatically declaring, *"I'm fine!"* when I was anything but.

But here's the thing: failure isn't the end of the world. It's not a dead-end but a detour sign on the road to success. There's always a new opportunity around the corner.

I've learned to see failures as life's way of course-correcting, a gentle (or sometimes, not so gentle) nudge towards the path I'm meant to tread. And no, this isn't me trying to sell you on some self-help mumbo-jumbo. This is me telling you the reality of my journey.

Every failure in my life, every stumble and fall, has been an invaluable learning opportunity. When I was accused of losing that fucking pot that Christmas morning, I learned I was not responsible for other people's inability to accept reality. When berated over the lunches I was "supposedly" not eating, I realized that some people will go to great lengths to avoid confronting their own issues.

Each of these failures was a stepping stone on my path to resilience. Like any person who spent hours trying to reach the next level in *Super Mario*, I learned that failure wasn't game over; it was just an opportunity to hit 'restart' and try again, armed with the knowledge of what didn't work the last time.

So, remember this: **every time life seems to shout 'game over,' look for the 'restart' button. Embrace failure, learn from it, and use it to fuel your journey to resilience. Because failure isn't a pit stop; it's just a scenic route to your destination. And hey, you might enjoy the view along the way.**

7. Setting Realistic Goals

Setting realistic, achievable goals can help build resilience. Having clear goals can provide a sense of purpose and direction, particularly during difficult times. It's essential to ensure your goals are realistic and within your control to avoid unnecessary disappointment and frustration.

Building resillence is not an overnight process. It's like a muscle – the more you exercise it, the stronger it gets. Every challenge you overcome, every mistake you learn from, and every setback you bounce back from helps to strengthen your resilience. It's a lifelong journey, but every step you take towards building strength is a step towards a healthier, more emotionally self-sufficient you.

Let's talk about goal-setting. When I say "goals," you might imagine climbing Mount Everest or becoming the next Beyoncé. While these are ambitious and exciting, they can also be overwhelming and feel distant.

We aim for what I call digestible goals. Imagine eating a whole pizza in one bite - a choking hazard, right? But if you slice it up, suddenly, it's much more manageable. It's the same with goals. For instance, one of my first digestible goals was to seek professional help. Instead of leaping headfirst into confronting every traumatic memory I had, I took it one step at a time. I sought a therapist, had an initial session, and then gradually opened up about my experiences. Each stage was a small victory, a slice of the whole pizza, if you will.

Another example was when I set a goal to maintain boundaries with my mother. I didn't just cut her off one day - that would have been too much, too fast. Instead, I started small. I limited phone calls, kept conversations shallow, and slowly distanced myself. With each step, I gained more control over my life.

There's incredible power in setting and achieving these smaller, realistic goals. Every time you reach one, you're making progress toward a more extensive plan and proving to yourself that

143

you can do it. It's like leveling up in a video game - each victory is progress, no matter how small. You're becoming more assertive, more resilient, and gaining confidence in your abilities.

Remember, this isn't a race, and there's no timeline that you need to follow. This is your journey, and it's all about making progress at your own pace. Healing is not linear, and it's not a 'one-size-fits-all' process.

It's important to celebrate these small victories, too. Have you bought yourself flowers? High five! Said no when you didn't feel like doing something? Awesome job! Managed to stand up for yourself in a challenging situation? Cue the confetti cannons! No matter how small they seem, these milestones are crucial in your resilience-building journey.

Finally, remember that Tokyo wasn't built in a day, nor is resilience. But with patience, perseverance, and a sense of humor, you can create a life you're proud to live. After all, as the great philosopher Drake once said, "*Started from the bottom, now we're here.*"

Cultivating Self-Love and Self-Worth

Emotional self-sufficiency also involves cultivating a sense of self-love and self-worth. This means recognizing your value and worth, independent of what others think or say about you. It's about learning to love and accept yourself just as you are, with all your strengths and flaws, and knowing that you are enough, just as you are.

Self-love and self-worth are interrelated concepts that form the cornerstone of emotional self-sufficiency. Cultivating these traits is a personal journey that requires time, effort, and, most importantly, patience:

1. Understanding Self-Love

Self-love isn't about narcissism or self-obsession. It's a state of appreciation for oneself that grows from actions that support our physical, psychological, and spiritual growth. It's about caring for our well-being and happiness and not sacrificing our needs to please others. Self-love means accepting ourselves as we are, acknowledging our achievements, and forgiving ourselves for our mistakes.

Practically, self-love can manifest in various ways: setting boundaries to maintain your mental and emotional health, saying no to work, love, or activities that deplete or harm you, and making choices that nurture your well-being and happiness.

You're flipping through Netflix, desperately searching for something to watch. Suddenly, you spot that infamous '80s movie, *The Breakfast Club*, and you're reminded of one of its iconic lines:

"We're all pretty bizarre. Some of us are just better at hiding it, that's all."

The beauty of this line is in its truth: we're all a unique blend of quirks, dreams, and insecurities. Self-love is about embracing this uniqueness wholeheartedly and unapologetically.

Self-love is akin to coming home after a long day and slipping into your favorite pair of worn-out pajamas. It's the comfort and acceptance of knowing every hole and stain and loving them regardless because they're yours. Just as those PJs hold stories of late-night ice cream spills, you, too, carry your own stories. And it's about embracing all of them - the glorious victories and the heart-wrenching defeats.

To translate self-love into actions, consider what you would do for a dear friend going through a tough time. You might take them out for a coffee, listen to their worries, reassure them of their worth, or sit with them in quiet understanding. Imagine extending that same compassion, experience, and patience toward yourself. That's self-love in action.

One aspect of self-love I had to learn was setting boundaries. It wasn't easy, but once I started to do it, I realized it was a powerful act of self-respect. Setting boundaries helped me create a safe space where I could control who and what could affect my mental and emotional well-being.

Remember when Buffy the Vampire Slayer had to stand up to her friends and make tough decisions for the greater good? That's what setting boundaries is like - sometimes you must be the "bad guy" to protect yourself and others. It's about asserting your needs in a relationship and having the self-respect to walk away if those needs aren't met.

Choosing self-love also means walking away from a job or relationship that no longer serves you, no matter how much you fear the unknown. It's like being trapped in a boring episode of *The Office* and having the courage to change the channel in search of something that makes you feel alive.

To sum up, self-love is a journey, not a destination. It's an ongoing process of setting boundaries, making conscious choices for your well-being, and appreciating your uniqueness. And it all starts with you deciding you're worth it, just like L'Oréal has been telling us for years.

2. Recognizing Your Self-Worth

Self-worth, on the other hand, is about understanding your value and recognizing that you deserve respect, love, and fulfillment, irrespective of your achievements, failures, or the opinions of others. It's the fundamental belief that you are valuable simply because you exist.

Cultivating self-worth means separating your worth from external factors. It's about challenging and changing the negative beliefs you have about yourself and replacing them with positive, empowering thoughts. It means no longer comparing yourself to others and recognizing that your worth is unique and cannot be diminished by anyone else.

Self-worth is like playing Mario Kart. You're on this journey, and these annoying banana peels are everywhere (we can call these our self-doubt or negativity). You're trying to dodge them, but sometimes you slip. But what do you do? You don't just stop and quit the game. You get back on track and keep going, power-up mushrooms and all. That's self-worth in action, understanding that a single slip doesn't define the entirety of your journey or your capability to win the race.

Cultivating self-worth was like learning a new language—the language of self-love. At first, it felt strange and foreign. There were sounds I couldn't pronounce and sentences I couldn't understand. After years of hearing and internalizing my mother's critical and abusive words, my inner voice became my worst critic.

But, like a determined student immersed in a foreign country, I started learning this new language. I began to replace the phrases of self-deprecation and doubt with words of self-compassion and confidence. I swapped out 'I can't' with 'I can' and 'I am not' with 'I am.' I started affirming my strengths and forgiving my weaknesses.

Remember when you used to repeat an iconic song lyric from a Britney Spears song repeatedly until you got it right? That's how affirmations work, except the lyrics are positive mantras about yourself. Repeating these mantras can help rewire your brain to believe in your worth and power.

Learning the language of self-love is not just about changing the way you talk to yourself but also how you treat yourself. It means establishing boundaries, taking care of your physical and mental health, and engaging in activities that you enjoy and that make you feel good. It means investing time and energy in YOU because you recognize that you are worth it. It's like treating yourself to a luxury spa day, except this spa day doesn't end—it becomes a lifestyle.

In my journey, recognizing my self-worth was a game-changer. It was the key that unlocked my potential and allowed me to break free from the confines of my past. It enabled me to redefine my identity and take control of my narrative. Ultimately, cultivating self-worth is about taking ownership of your life. It's about embracing who you are, flaws and all, and recognizing that you are a person of worth, deserving of love, respect, and happiness. Remember, you're the main character in your life story, so don't play a supporting role. Stand in the spotlight and take a bow because you, dear reader, are worth it.

3. **Practical Steps for Cultivating Self-Love and Self-Worth**

There are numerous ways to cultivate self-love and self-worth. Here are a few practical steps:

Affirmations: You remember the "I'm good enough, I'm smart enough, and doggone it, people like me!"

sketch from *Saturday Night Live*, right? Affirmations are like that, but less '90s cheese and more personal empowerment. They're like your personal cheer squad, lifting you up when you are feeling down. And don't worry, they don't have to be public declarations. You can whisper them to yourself in the mirror, write them down in a journal, or even set them as reminders on your phone. The key is consistency because affirmations need daily care, much like a Tamagotchi.

Self-Care: By all means, pamper yourself if that makes you happy. Think of self-care as anything that recharges your emotional batteries. Maybe it's reading your favorite book, doing yoga, or blasting Kelly Clarkson's "Stronger" on repeat (no judgment here).

Setting Boundaries: This is one of the most challenging yet crucial steps. It's about asserting your needs and values and not allowing others to overstep or disrespect them. Picture it like building a fort when you were a kid. Inside that fort, you're safe. You control who can enter and what they can bring inside. Outside of the fort might be a sea of lava (or, in this case, toxic behaviors), but within your walls, you're safe and sound. Saying 'no' can be daunting, but remember, every time you say 'no' to something that drains you, you're saying 'yes' to your well-being.

Seeking Professional Help: Sometimes, self-help measures aren't enough, and that's okay. Seeking professional help is not a sign of defeat. It's actually a courageous step toward healing. Therapists and counselors are there to guide, support, and equip you with the tools you need to fight your battles. Remember, it's okay to ask for help. As the Beatles so wisely sang, "We get by with a little help from our friends"—sometimes, those friends are therapists.

Incorporating these practices into your daily routine might seem overwhelming initially, but remember, you're not alone in this journey. Whether through therapy, a support group, or the love of understanding friends or partners, there are people ready to help you cultivate self-love and self-worth.

Developing Emotional Intelligence

A big part of emotional self-sufficiency is emotional intelligence - the ability to understand and manage your own emotions, as well as to empathize with the feelings of others. When emotionally intelligent, you can navigate complex situations more effectively, communicate better, and build stronger relationships. And most importantly, you better understand what you need to be happy and fulfilled.

Emotional intelligence, often abbreviated as EQ, involves four critical skills:

1. Self-Awareness:

This is the ability to recognize your own emotions as they happen and understand how they affect your thoughts and behaviors. It's about knowing what you are feeling and why. This includes an awareness of your strengths and weaknesses, values, and drives. Self-awareness is the foundation of emotional intelligence because without understanding our own emotions, it will be harder to understand the feelings of others.

Think of self-awareness as the introspective superhero inside of you. It doesn't wear a cape, leap tall buildings, or even have a catchy theme song, but trust me, it's just as powerful as any comic book character. Without a strong sense of self-awareness, we can become lost in the narratives woven by others. We become like actors in a play, adhering to a script that doesn't reflect our true selves.

Self-awareness goes beyond merely recognizing if you're feeling happy or sad, angry or calm. It's about deciphering why a specific event or interaction stirs certain emotions. For example, why does your heart rate spike when your boss sends you an unexpected email, or why do you feel sad when you see a parent cheering on their child at a park?

In my case, I had to dig deep to understand my reactions. Why did I jump at sudden noises, or why would a seemingly innocuous comment trigger a flood of anger? Understanding that these were not typical reactions but symptoms of my traumatic past was crucial to my self-awareness journey.

Moreover, self-awareness allows you to recognize your strengths and weaknesses. We all have them, and they're not something to be ashamed of. Instead, they're opportunities for growth and improvement. For instance, I discovered that I was empathetic—a strength that allowed me to connect with others deeply. But on the flip side, my tendency to avoid conflict at all costs was a weakness that often kept me from standing up for myself.

Finally, self-awareness is the compass that directs you to your values and drives. These core principles guide your actions, decisions, and relationships. Understanding that my purpose was no longer about seeking validation from others but nurturing my well-being was a pivotal shift in my healing journey.

Understanding your emotions, acknowledging your strengths and weaknesses, and identifying your values and drives are like adding entries to your personal manual. It's a guidebook written by you—a tool that equips you to navigate life's challenges with resilience, compassion, and humor.

Self-awareness isn't a destination—it's a journey. It's about continually learning, growing, and evolving. It's about being brave enough to face your true self and say, "*I see you, I understand you, and I accept you.*" And believe me, there's no greater superhero power than that.

2. Self-Management:

This is regulating and controlling your emotions, especially in stressful situations. Instead of letting your emotions control you, you handle them. You can adapt to changing circumstances without becoming overwhelmed. This doesn't mean suppressing what you're feeling but acknowledging those feelings and finding ways to manage them. For instance, if you're feeling angry, self-management involves recognizing that anger, understanding why you're feeling it, and then channeling it positively.

Take, for instance, the uncontainable rage I'd feel whenever my mom went on one of her accusatory tirades. I would have exploded in the past, fueling the already raging fire. But with self-management, I began to view my emotions like waves on an ocean shore—ebb and flow, crash and recede. Like a surfer, I learned to ride these waves, not attempting to stop or control them but navigating through them.

So, the anger? That red-hot, festering ball of fury? It was no longer a destructive force that would consume me and everything in its path. Instead, I took a deep breath. I paused. I acknowledged the anger bubbling inside me but did not let it spill over. I did not suppress it either but allowed myself to feel it fully, just like tasting a super spicy hot sauce that makes you want to dance, scream, and curse all at once.

Understanding the origin of this anger was like reading the most complex, intricate mystery novel. Each feeling was a clue, leading me deeper into the labyrinth of my past. I asked myself, "Why am I feeling this anger? Is it truly because of the current situation, or is it an echo from the past? How does it serve me?" Often, I found that my anger was a masked defense mechanism, a response ingrained in me since childhood to protect myself from my mother's hurtful narratives.

Channeling this anger positively was like redirecting a raging river into a hydroelectric dam—it became a source of power, not destruction. For instance, when I felt that familiar surge of anger, I began to channel it into constructive outlets—writing in my journal, going for a run, or even creating colorful, abstract paintings that embodied my emotions. It was almost as if each brushstroke on the canvas or pounding footstep on the pavement reaffirmed my control over my emotional state.

Self-management isn't a destination but a journey that requires constant practice, patience, and, above all, self-compassion. It means allowing yourself to stumble, fall, and then rise again. And remember, it's okay if you can't always tame the storm of your emotions. Sometimes, it's about learning to dance in the rain, knowing you can weather it.

Next time you watch the latest episode of *The Real Housewives* and find yourself seething because one of the characters reminds you of your mother, remember to take a deep breath. Pause. Recognize your anger, understand it, and channel it positively. And hey, who knows? The subsequent great art or groundbreaking novel lies on the other side of that anger. It's all in the channeling.

3. Social Awareness:

This is the ability to understand and pick up on the emotions of others and understand what is really going on. This involves empathy - understanding others' feelings and seeing things from their perspective. Empathy helps us to connect with others on a deep level and builds better relationships.

Picture, if you will, an "emotional radar." It scans the room, picking up on subtle cues - a sigh here, a slump of the shoulders there, a grimace, a frown. This radar helps us gauge the emotional temperature around us, allowing us to interact more effectively and empathetically with others. Social awareness is that radar, a key component in developing and maintaining meaningful relationships.

Now, you might wonder why social awareness is essential, especially for someone who grew up with an emotionally manipulative parent. When you've been repeatedly subjected to manipulation and gaslighting, your emotional radar can get a bit skewed. You might become hyper-alert to potential threats, seeing malice where none exists. Or, on the other hand, you might downplay or ignore signs of potential harm, a holdover from years of enduring abusive behavior.

But let's take a moment to step back and consider the bigger picture. Social awareness isn't just about deciphering others' emotions but understanding their experiences and perspectives. It's about fostering empathy, a powerful feeling that connects us to others and inspires compassion. Empathy isn't just understanding that someone is feeling sad; it's imagining how they might feel and sharing their emotional experience.

Consider a time when you shared a painful experience with a friend. Did they shrug it off and tell you to "*just get over it*," or did they listen, acknowledge your feelings, and offer comfort? The latter is empathy in action—a warm, comforting presence that tells you, "*I see you, I hear you, and I'm here for you.*" Developing social awareness and empathy becomes invaluable as you journey towards healing and self-love. It fosters healthier relationships where you can offer and receive emotional support. It can also help break the cycle of abuse and neglect, replacing it with a cycle of understanding, compassion, and connection.

However, it's also important to remember this: empathy is not about taking on others' emotional baggage. You are not responsible for fixing others' problems or healing their wounds. Empathy is about understanding and acknowledgment, not self-sacrifice. After all, you can't pour from an empty cup—you must also ensure your emotional well-being.

As you navigate your emotional landscape, remember that seeking help is okay. A therapist or counselor can offer valuable guidance, providing tools and strategies to develop social awareness and empathy. So, let's continue this journey together, fostering understanding and connection, one empathetic interaction at a time.

4. Relationship Management:

This is building and maintaining good relationships, communicating clearly, influencing others, and managing conflict. It's about knowing how to apply your knowledge of your own emotions and those of others to create positive interactions and maintain strong relationships.

Imagine yourself as the conductor of a symphony. Each instrument represents a different relationship in your life. The violins could be your close friends, the cellos, your family, the brass, your colleagues, and so on. Your job, as the conductor, is to create beautiful music and ensure that every instrument plays in harmony. This is relationship management.

This begins with understanding the emotions of others, or empathy. Think of it as the sheet music that guides your interactions. When a friend feels down (a violin's low, mournful tones), you respond with kindness and support. When a family member is jubilant (the exuberant call of a trumpet), you share in their joy. This emotional attunement helps to foster a deeper, more meaningful connection.

Now, let's consider communication - the baton in your hand. A conductor uses their baton to set the tempo and bring in different instruments at the right time. In the same way, effective communication in relationships involves knowing when to speak, when to listen, and how to express your thoughts and feelings clearly. A well-timed word of encouragement or an attentive ear can make all the difference in a relationship.

Influence is another vital aspect of relationship management. No, I'm not talking about being an Instagram Influencer with many followers, hanging on your every hashtag. Influence in relationships is about encouraging positive changes and resolving conflicts. You're the conductor, remember? Sometimes, you must guide the trombones to play a little softer or encourage the flutes to take the lead.

Lastly, but certainly not least, is conflict management. A symphony is not only smooth sailing. There will be discordant notes and clashing harmonies. The same goes for relationships. Conflicts are natural and, if handled well, can lead to growth and deeper understanding. As the conductor, it's your role to address these discordances, to transform them from cacophony to symphony. This might mean apologizing when you're wrong, standing up for yourself when you're right, and always striving for fairness and understanding.

You're not just a member of the orchestra. You're the maestro, the conductor guiding the symphony of your life. You can create a beautiful

159

melody of meaningful and healthy relationships through empathy, clear communication, influence, and conflict management.

Building emotional intelligence only happens after some time. It requires time, patience, and practice. You can start by simply paying attention to your emotions and the emotions of those around you. Notice how you react to different situations. Pay attention to what triggers strong emotions in you, and think about how you might manage those emotions more effectively. Similarly, try to put yourself in other people's shoes and understand their feelings. This can help you to respond more effectively in social situations and build stronger relationships.

Developing emotional intelligence can make a big difference in your journey toward emotional self-sufficiency. It can help you to understand and manage your emotions, navigate social situations more effectively, and build stronger, healthier relationships. And most importantly, it can help you to create a more fulfilling, happier life.

Practicing Mindfulness and Self-Reflection

Emotional self-sufficiency also involves mindfulness and self-reflection. Mindfulness is about being fully present in the moment. It's about shifting your focus away from past regrets or future anxieties and immersing yourself fully in the here and now. This doesn't mean that you ignore your past or don't plan for your future, but instead that you don't let them dominate your thoughts to the point where they detract from your current experiences.

Practicing mindfulness can take many forms, from meditation and yoga to simply taking a few moments each day to focus on your breath, listen to the sounds around you, or feel the sensations in your body. Even mundane tasks, like washing the dishes or taking a shower, can become exercises in mindfulness if you focus entirely on what you're doing and experiencing.

The beauty of mindfulness is that it allows you to better understand your thoughts and feelings rather than being swept away by them. This can be particularly helpful when you're dealing with difficult emotions. Instead of trying to suppress or ignore these feelings, mindfulness encourages you to acknowledge and accept them, understanding that they are part of your current experience but do not define you or your future.

Embracing Self-Reflection

Self-reflection, however, is about taking the time to consciously think about your thoughts, feelings, and experiences. It's about asking yourself, "*Why did I react that way?*" "*What were the underlying emotions behind my response?*" or "*What can I learn from this situation?*"

Self-reflection allows you to gain a deeper understanding of yourself. It helps you to recognize patterns in your thoughts and behaviors, identify areas where you may want to make changes, and understand how your past experiences have shaped you. While self-reflection can sometimes be uncomfortable, especially when it involves facing brutal truths about yourself, it is vital to emotional self-sufficiency. It enables you to take responsibility for your own growth and development instead of placing the blame on others or external circumstances.

Incorporating mindfulness and self-reflection into your daily routine doesn't require a considerable time commitment, but it does require consistency. Even just a few minutes each day can make a significant difference. The more you practice, the better you'll understand and manage your emotions, ultimately leading to a stronger sense of self-sufficiency.

The Journey to Inner Happiness

The road to self-sufficiency and inner happiness can be challenging. It's paved with self-reflection, introspection, and sometimes painful realizations. But every step on this journey brings you closer to a life of fulfillment and inner peace.

The journey to inner happiness began when I started acknowledging my past, my scars, and my vulnerabilities. I began to learn more about myself, my needs, and my desires. And then I started prioritizing them. I set boundaries and learned to say no. I meditated, read self-help books, and, most importantly, allowed myself to feel.

Finding happiness within doesn't mean you won't experience negative emotions. On the contrary, it means you acknowledge them, accept them, and learn from them. It means you can feel sad, angry, or frustrated without letting these emotions take control. Talking about a journey often conjures up images of a long and winding road with ups and downs. Your journey to inner happiness is no different.

Here's a deeper look into the processes and steps involved:

1. Acknowledgment and Acceptance of Past Hurts

Acknowledging your past, scars, and vulnerabilities is like standing at the start line of your journey. This involves looking back on your experiences and recognizing how they've shaped you but without judgment or resentment. It's about accepting your past as a part of your story but not the entire narrative. Acknowledgment and acceptance of past hurt is like standing at your journey's start line. This can be one of the most challenging steps as it involves revisiting painful experiences and their emotions.

Let's break it down further:

Recognizing Your Experiences: This involves consciously recalling your past experiences, particularly those that left a deep emotional imprint on you. It could be events from your childhood, like parental neglect or abuse, or experiences from your adult life, like toxic relationships or personal failures. Recognizing these experiences is about objectively identifying them without delving into the emotions they evoke just yet.

Understanding Their Impact: Once you've identified these key experiences, the next step is understanding their impact on your life. How did these experiences shape your attitudes, behaviors, and responses? For example, in my case, the neglect and abuse from my mother led to anger issues, the inability to form healthy relationships and a constant state of survival mode. This step involves deep introspection and reflection.

Acknowledging Your Scars and Vulnerabilities: This is where you start connecting your past experiences to your present state. Your scars are your emotional wounds, the pain and hurt you carry. Your vulnerabilities are sensitive spots, aspects of your life that can easily trigger negative emotions. Acknowledging them involves admitting they exist and understanding that they are a part of who you are.

Letting Go of Judgment and Resentment: This step is crucial for healing. It involves looking at your past without judgment or resentment. It's about letting go of blame – whether it's blaming others or blaming yourself. It's about understanding that everyone, including your parents, acted based on their awareness, knowledge, and ability.

Accepting Your Past: This is the final and most crucial step. It's about accepting your past as a part of your life story. It doesn't define you, but it has shaped you. It's about understanding that while you can't change past events, you have control over your present and future. Acceptance is not about forgetting your past but about making peace with it.

QUESTIONS

What are some experiences in your past that you find difficult to think about?

How have these experiences shaped who you are today?

Who or what do you blame for these past hurts?

How can you work on letting go of that blame?

EXCERCISE:

*Write down 3-5 past hurts, and for each, write down
how it has affected you. Then write down a step you
can take to begin accepting and integrating each
experience.*

2. Understanding Self

Self-discovery is the next step on this road. It involves understanding who you are at your core - your values, strengths, weaknesses, and passions. This understanding allows you to better articulate your needs and desires and fosters a stronger sense of self-identity and self-worth.

Let's delve a little deeper into the concept of 'Understanding Self':

Exploring Your Values: Values are the principles and standards of behavior that we hold dear. They are deeply embedded and influence every aspect of our lives - from how we interact with others to our decisions. Exploring your values requires reflection and honesty. Ask yourself questions like "*What matters most to me?*" or "*What principles guide my actions and decisions?*" These questions can help you better understand your core values and how they shape your identity.

Recognizing Your Strengths and Weaknesses: Understanding yourself also means recognizing your strengths and weaknesses. It's about acknowledging what you're good at and where to improve. This step requires introspection and a level of self-awareness. Identifying your strengths can boost your self-confidence and help you realize your potential while acknowledging your weaknesses can highlight areas for growth and development.

Discovering Your Passions: Your passions can offer significant insight into who you are at your core. They're the things you love to do, the activities that light you up and make you lose track of time. Discovering your passions can reveal what motivates you, what interests you, and what brings you joy. This understanding can guide you towards more fulfilling experiences and align your life with what truly matters to you.

Articulating Your Needs and Desires: You'll be better equipped to articulate your needs and desires as you gain a deeper understanding of yourself. This involves expressing what you want and need from yourself and your relationships. It's a crucial part of self-assertion and maintaining healthy boundaries.

Cultivating Self-Worth: You'll be better positioned to cultivate self-worth with a deeper understanding of your values, strengths, weaknesses, and passions. Self-worth stems from recognizing your inherent value, independent of external validation. It means knowing that you matter and are enough, just as you are.

EXCERCISE:

Values Clarification

List down as many values as you can think of and prioritize your top 5. Reflect on whether your actions align with these values.

What are your core values?

What are some strengths that you're proud of?

What are some weaknesses that you'd like to work on?

3. Prioritizing Self

After understanding yourself, it's time to prioritize yourself. For some, this could mean setting boundaries and learning to say no when things don't align with your values. For others, taking up activities that bring joy and peace, like yoga, meditation, or reading. Once you've understood your needs, values, strengths, and weaknesses, the next step is to start giving those elements the importance they deserve. Prioritizing yourself is not about selfishness, as some might mistakenly believe. It is about recognizing that your well-being matters, and you are entitled to devote time and energy to maintaining it.

Let's delve deeper into what this entails:

Honoring Your Values: Your values are the guiding principles that dictate your behavior and actions. They are profoundly personal and range from honesty and compassion to ambition and self-expression. Prioritizing yourself means living a life aligned with these values. If authenticity is a value you hold dear, this could translate into being open and truthful in your relationships, even when it's complicated. On the other hand, if personal growth is a key value, this might involve seeking out new learning experiences and opportunities for self-improvement.

Investing in Self-Care: Self-care involves activities and practices you regularly engage in to reduce stress and maintain your well-being. This could be physical self-care, like exercising, sleeping well, or eating healthy foods. It could also be emotional self-care, like journaling, therapy, or speaking with a trusted friend. Mindful activities like yoga and meditation also fall into this category, as they can help reduce stress and enhance mental clarity. Self-care could be as simple as setting aside time to do things you enjoy, like reading a good book, exploring nature, or indulging in a favorite hobby. Prioritizing self-care is a fundamental aspect of prioritizing yourself.

Affirming Your Self-Worth: Lastly, prioritizing yourself involves affirming your self-worth. This means acknowledging your strengths, celebrating your achievements (no matter how small), and cultivating positive self-talk. It involves dismantling the internalized negative beliefs that may have been instilled by past traumas or adverse experiences and replacing them with positive, empowering thoughts about yourself. You deserve love, respect, and happiness, and it's important to remind yourself of this regularly.

REFLECTIVE
QUESTION

In what areas of life could you better align your actions with your values?

Continuous Learning and Growth

The phrase "continuous learning and growth" might sound like a lofty ideal, but it's actually a simple commitment to being open and adaptable. It's acknowledging that life is an evolving journey filled with lessons and opportunities for personal development.

Being open to growth means accepting that you are a work in progress. It's about embracing that we're never 'finished' individuals, and there is always room for development, no matter our age or circumstance. It's about seeking new experiences and opportunities, taking risks, and stepping out of your comfort zone. Every experience, both positive and negative, offers a chance for growth and self-discovery.

Constant Learning About Yourself and The World

This involves actively seeking knowledge, understanding, and wisdom. It's about introspection and self-reflection. Understanding yourself better: your motivations, your triggers, your strengths, and areas for improvement. But it's also about being curious about the world around you and understanding different cultures, perspectives, and ideas. All these contribute to a richer, more nuanced view of life and a better understanding of your place.

Think about your life as an uncharted map. There are hidden treasures, labyrinthine twists and turns, and countless landscapes to explore. The same is true for your internal landscape. Your emotions, thoughts, and experiences form a complex terrain you could explore for a lifetime. Self-discovery is not a one-time event; it's a continuous process. Take the time to understand what makes you, well, you.

Motivations: What drives you? Is it the desire for success, the need for love, or perhaps the pursuit of an enduring passion?

Triggers: Knowing what sets you off is crucial for self-regulation. The better you understand your triggers, the easier it is to navigate emotionally challenging situations.

Strengths: Understanding your skills and talents helps you operate from a place of confidence.

Areas for Improvement: Nobody's perfect, and acknowledging your weaknesses is not a sign of defeat but an opportunity for growth.

As important as it is to know yourself, it's equally vital to understand the world around you. Your perspective is shaped not just by your internal world but also by your interactions with the external world. So, unplug from the self occasionally and tune into the global frequency.

Cultural Sensitivity: The more you learn about other cultures, the more you appreciate the tapestry of human experience. This isn't just about avoiding social faux pas; it's about enriching your understanding of human diversity.

176

Perspective-taking: This involves understanding situations from multiple viewpoints. You don't have to agree, but understanding different perspectives can enrich your own.

Curiosity about World Events: Keeping up to date with current events offers more than small talk material; it gives you context for the state of the world, helping you understand your place in it.

The more you know about yourself, the better you'll understand others. Conversely, the more you see the world and people around you, the deeper your self-understanding will be. This creates a symbiotic relationship between self-awareness and world awareness.

Empathy and Emotional Intelligence: One of the most remarkable benefits of this dual learning approach is enhancing your emotional intelligence. By understanding both yourself and others, you can navigate social landscapes with more empathy and efficacy.

Constant learning doesn't have to be a formal endeavor. It's as simple as pausing to reflect at the end of the day, reading a book that challenges you, or even striking up a conversation with someone from a different background. Turn everyday moments into learning opportunities.

By embracing a lifelong learning approach that encompasses both personal and global perspectives, you enrich your life and contribute to a more understanding and compassionate world. In the grand tapestry of life, learning is the thread that weaves all experiences together into a coherent, meaningful whole.

QUESTIONS

How open are you to new experiences?

Can you recall an instance where you stepped out of your comfort zone?

Striving to Be the Best Version of Yourself

Let's get one thing straight: pursuing the best version of yourself doesn't mean chasing after an unattainable idea of perfection. That's a one-way ticket to Burnoutsville. Instead, think of it as a journey—your personal "road less traveled," if you will. It's a quest to unlock the best parts of you, given your unique set of circumstances, talents, and limitations.

Think of yourself as a diamond in the rough. Your true brilliance may be obscured by life's pressures and challenges, but trust me, it's in there. The first step is acknowledging that you have untapped potential. This is different for everyone. It could be a talent you've never nurtured, a skill you've never developed, or a boundary you've never set. Recognizing your potential is like finding North on your internal compass; it sets the direction for your journey.

Once you've got your bearings, the next part is walking the walk. This involves setting achievable goals for yourself. These can be small, like finally cleaning out that one junk drawer, or monumental, like going back to school to switch careers. The size of the goal isn't what matters; it's the act of setting it and then taking steps, however small, to achieve it.

Remember, your body is the vehicle on this road trip, so regular maintenance is vital. This doesn't mean you have to look like a fitness guru or survive on a diet of kale and optimism. It just means regular exercise to the best of your ability, eating balanced meals, and getting enough sleep. Small changes often yield surprising benefits, like increased energy and better mental clarity.

Just like you wouldn't ignore the warning lights on your car's dashboard, you shouldn't overlook your emotional warning signals either. Feeling perpetually stressed, anxious, or down are signs that something needs your attention. This might mean seeking professional help or discussing your feelings with trusted friends or family. Emotional self-care is not a luxury; it's a necessity for being the best version of yourself. Investing in your mental well-being often gets pushed to the wayside. Most people promise to do it right after they 'get through this busy period,' which never seems to end. Mental well-being is about keeping your mind sharp and your inner life rich. This could be as simple as reading regularly, engaging in stimulating conversations or even taking up a hobby that challenges you.

Lastly, but most importantly, none of this works without a good dose of self-love. Treat yourself with the same kindness and respect you'd offer to someone you care deeply for. This isn't narcissism; it's necessary for positive personal development. Acknowledge your achievements, however minor. Forgive yourself for your setbacks, and learn from them. You're a work in progress, and that's perfectly okay.

In short, becoming the best version of yourself is an ongoing process that requires a balanced investment in your body, heart, and mind. It's not about reaching some imaginary pinnacle of perfection; it's about continually climbing, learning, and improving while enjoying the view. So lace up those hiking boots; your mountain is waiting.

EXCERCISE:

Growth Plan

Write down one area in your life where you'd like to grow. Create a list of steps to achieve this and a timeline.

Finding Joy in the Little Moments, Peace in Chaos, and Love Within Yourself

Finding happiness within isn't about grand moments of joy or achievement (though those are great, too!). It's about appreciating the small moments: a beautiful sunrise, a good book, a heartfelt conversation with a friend, or a delicious meal. It's about finding peace amidst the chaos of life and learning to be comfortable with solitude and quiet.

It's also about cultivating self-love and self-compassion. It's about acknowledging your worth and loving yourself, flaws and all. Self-love is crucial to inner happiness, as it forms the foundation for a positive self-image and healthy self-esteem. Remember, your journey to inner happiness is personal and unique. It won't look like anyone else's journey, and that's okay. It's not about comparing or competing. It's about owning your path, embracing your progress, and cherishing every step you take toward a more fulfilling, happier life. Every action, every stumble, every victory is a part of your story. And your tale is beautiful, filled with resilience, growth, and an ever-evolving journey toward inner happiness.

REFLECTIVE
QUESTIONS

What are some small moments that bring you joy?

How do you cultivate peace within yourself?

Personal Growth and Self-Improvement: The Path to Fulfillment

Self-sufficiency is closely linked to personal growth and self-improvement. Being self-sufficient means taking responsibility for your life, including your development. But self-love isn't about being selfish or self-absorbed. It's about respecting yourself, knowing your worth, and investing in personal growth.

This can take many forms. For some, it might mean returning to school or picking up a new hobby. For others, it might mean seeking therapy or practicing mindfulness. It involved a lot of writing, self-reflection, and even developing a children's book series to heal my inner child.

Remember, personal growth is not a race. It's a journey. And it's okay to take it one step at a time. Your journey will be unique, filled with successes and setbacks. But every step you take towards self-improvement is a step towards a more fulfilling life. Everyone moves at their own pace, so it's essential to understand your rhythm. You can't compare your journey with anyone else's, and that's perfectly okay. There might be days when you make great strides forward and days when you don't feel like you've moved. That's part of the journey; it doesn't mean you're failing. On the contrary, it's a sign that you're human and something to celebrate. One step at a time.

When I say "one step at a time," I mean focusing on small, attainable goals rather than huge, overwhelming ones. If your goal is to cultivate more self-love, start with something simple like practicing daily affirmations or dedicating ten minutes a day to self-care. Every small victory counts and these little steps can lead to significant changes. Part of taking it one step at a time is understanding that mistakes are a natural part of the journey. In fact, they're not just part of the journey; they're essential to it. Every mistake is a learning opportunity. It's a chance to grow, improve, and understand who you are and what you want from life.

Ultimately, the journey to personal growth and self-improvement isn't about reaching a final destination. It's about the lessons you learn, the person you become, and the happiness you find.

So, no matter how long it takes, remember to celebrate each step forward, no matter how small, because each step is a step towards a more fulfilling life.

REFLECTIVE
QUESTIONS

In what ways are you already practicing self-love?

What are some realistic goals you can set for your self-improvement journey?

SMART Goals

Create a SMART (Specific, Measurable, Achievable, Relevant, Time-bound) goal related to your personal growth. Outline the steps you need to achieve it.

CHAPTER 10

TA-DAH!

"You've always had the power, my dear, you just had to learn it for yourself."

*- Glinda the Good Witch,
The Wizard of Oz*

Well, here we are—the end of our book, yet the beginning of so many beautiful, new narratives for you. This isn't just a story about trauma, neglect, abuse, or a narcissistic mother; it's about resilience, healing, and reclaiming your life. Our journey together might end with this chapter, but your personal journey toward growth, healing, and empowerment is just taking off. We've dissected my life experiences, each an unsightly slice of a painful past yet a testament to strength and survival. We've journeyed through valleys, trekked up mountains, and swum through rivers metaphorically and emotionally. Take a moment to consider the following reflection questions:

REFLECTIVE
QUESTIONS

How have your views on your past experiences changed after reading this book?

What are the most important lessons you've learned about yourself?

What steps are you planning to take immediately after reading this book?

What are your long-term goals for healing and personal growth?

The Road Ahead: Your Unfolding Journey

The journey toward reclaiming your life is perpetual, filled with twists, turns, and lessons yet to be learned. So, what can you expect on the road ahead?

You'll experience seasons of harvest where everything feels abundant, and then there will be winter periods where personal growth has come to a halt. Both are natural and necessary for your evolution.

You might sometimes feel like you're backtracking, circling, or even at a dead-end. But remember, it's not about the destination. It's about the journey. You're making progress if you keep putting one foot before the other.

REFLECTIVE
QUESTIONS

How prepared are you for the different seasons of life?

Write down the potential challenges you might face on your journey.

The Importance of Revisiting Your Goals

As you evolve, so will your goals and aspirations. Don't be rigid; allow your dreams to adapt as you grow. Your relationships will also evolve as you do. Some will grow stronger; others might fade away, and that's okay. The key is to foster relationships that contribute positively to your life.

EXCERCISE:

Relationship Audit
Make a list of the five people you spend the most time with. Next to each name, write down how they impact your life—positively or negatively. Consider how you might want to change your relationship dynamics moving forward.

Please promise to be kind to yourself along the way. There will be moments of self-doubt or times when you feel you've veered off the path. Self-compassion should be your go-to in these times. You've already come so far, and though the journey ahead may be long, remember that every step is a victory. Embrace the uncertainty and complexity of life; it's where you'll find your deepest learnings and most profound joys.

Remember, there's a vast universe inside you waiting to be explored, and it's high time we stopped focusing on distractions and started appreciating the cosmos. Your past might be a part of your universe, but it certainly isn't the whole.

You've got this. Your journey is unique, your strength is unparalleled, and your future is bright. Here's to breaking free, living, loving, and, most importantly, laughing. And in the spirit of continuing your journey, I'll leave you with another empowering quote:

"Do not wait to strike till the iron is hot; but make it hot by striking."

—William Butler Yeats

ADDITIONAL TOOLS & RESOURCES

Since writing this book, my personal journey has been far from static. I've delved deeper into some of the practices I've shared, finding new layers of understanding and application that have enriched my life. I've also discovered new tools, strategies, and wisdom that I wish I could've included. Healing and personal growth are continual processes, and I hope you'll remain a lifelong student of your own well-being, just as I am of mine.

Recommended Reading

- **"The Body Keeps the Score"** by Bessel van der Kolk

  This groundbreaking book explores how trauma affects not just the mind but the body as well. It provides scientific insights interwoven with real-life stories and offers holistic approaches to healing.

- **"Daring Greatly"** by Brené Brown

  Brené Brown's research on vulnerability and courage has revolutionized our understanding of these concepts. This book will inspire you to embrace vulnerability as a source of strength.

- **"Attached"** by Amir Levine and Rachel Heller

  Ever feel like you're caught in a cycle of relationship highs and lows? "Attached" will help you understand your attachment style and how it affects your relationships. It's a game-changer!

- **"Healing the Fragmented Selves of Trauma Survivors"** by Janina Fisher

  This book sheds light on overcoming traumatic responses. It's like having a wise friend explain the complexities of trauma and the paths to healing.

- **"When the Body Says No"** *by Gabor Maté*

  Dr. Maté explores the mind-body link and its critical role in healing from stress and trauma. It's compelling and full of real-world wisdom.

- **"The Gifts of Imperfection"** *by Brené Brown*

  If you liked "Daring Greatly", you will love this one! Brené Brown digs deep into embracing our flaws and imperfections, showing us the way to live a wholehearted life.

Supportive Online Communities

- **7 Cups**

    Need someone to talk to? 7 Cups connects you to caring listeners for free emotional support. It's like a friend who's always there, anytime you need to get something off your chest.

- **BetterHelp**

    It offers online counseling with licensed therapists who specialize in issues like trauma, anxiety, and relationships. It's a convenient way to get professional help without leaving home.

- **TalkSpace**

    TalkSpace makes therapy accessible and affordable with professional online counseling tailored to your needs. It's another cozy corner of the internet where support is just a click away.

- **RAINN (Rape, Abuse & Incest National Network)**

    RAINN offers support to sexual assault survivors and educates the public about sexual violence. It's a safe space to find help and understand more about sexual trauma.

Websites for Wellness and Mental Health

- **mindful.org**

  A fantastic resource for articles, guided practices, and tips on mindfulness, which can be instrumental in both daily well-being and long-term healing.

- **PsychCentral.com**

  This website offers a myriad of articles, quizzes, and expert opinions on psychology, mental health, and wellness.

- **The National Child Traumatic Stress Network (NCTSN)**

  Provides a wealth of information and resources on childhood trauma, its impact, and strategies for healing and prevention.

- **Anxiety and Depression Association of America (ADAA)**

  Offers valuable resources, including support groups, therapists, and treatments, for those dealing with anxiety and depression.

- **Mental Health America (MHA)**

  MHA provides resources, information, and assistance to those dealing with mental health conditions. It's a comprehensive guide to understanding various aspects of mental health.

- **The Mighty**

  This is a digital health community created to empower and connect people facing health challenges and disabilities. It's a supportive community where experiences are shared, and advice is given.

Courses for Further Learning

- **"Self-Compassion"**, by Kristin Neff on Udemy

  Self-compassion is more than a buzzword—it's a life skill. Kristin Neff's course offers practical ways to develop self-compassion, which can be a game-changer in your journey toward well-being.

- **"The Science of Well-Being"** by Yale University on Coursera

  This course will help you unlock the secrets to happiness by exploring what psychological science says about living a more satisfying life.

- **"Understanding and Healing Trauma"** on Udemy

  This course delves into understanding and working through trauma, providing insights and strategies to build resilience and embark on a healing journey.

- **"Trauma-Informed Care: Transforming Treatment and Lives"** *on Edx*

  Explore how trauma-informed care can alter the course of lives and treatment outcomes. It's your ticket to deeper understanding and positive change.

- **"Learning How to Learn"** *on Coursera*
  This course teaches you about optimizing your learning process, which can be especially helpful when exploring new healing and self-help practices. It's a smooth ride into becoming a more effective learner.

Apps for Healing & Mindfulness

- **Calm**

  This app offers guided meditations and sleep stories to help improve mindfulness and sleep quality.

- **MyFitnessPal**

  While it's commonly known as a diet and exercise app, MyFitnessPal can be an excellent resource for tracking habits that contribute to your well-being.

- **Headspace**

  This app offers a variety of mindfulness exercises and guided meditations to help you stay present and cultivate peace in your everyday life.

- **Moodpath**

  Moodpath is your pocket-sized mental health companion. Whether you are facing a rough patch or have concerns about your mental health, the app's goal is to support you through it all.

- **Insight Timer**

  Here's another app with thousands of free guided meditations, music tracks, and talks about mindfulness. It's like a little peace haven in your pocket.

- **Daylio**

  Daylio enables you to keep a private journal without having to type a single line. It's a little companion to help you reflect and keep track of your mood and activities.

Engaging Podcasts

- **"The Happiness Lab"** with Dr. Laurie Santos

  In this podcast, Dr. Laurie Santos reveals the latest scientific research on happiness and shows practical ways to live a more fulfilling and contented life.

- **"The Healing Trauma Podcast"**

  This podcast offers insights and interviews from various experts on trauma and recovery. It's a beacon of hope and understanding for anyone navigating through their trauma.

- **"Unlocking Us"** with Brené Brown

  Brené Brown dives into conversations about the human experience. It's like having a cup of coffee with someone who truly understands the ups and downs of life.

- **"Where Should We Begin?"** with Esther Perel

  Listen to real couples therapy sessions with renowned relationship therapist Esther Perel. It's a window into the complex world of relationships and the human psyche.

Your journey doesn't end when you close the cover of this book; it's merely a new chapter in your life story. Consider these resources as potential companions for the road ahead, helping you navigate through the complexities and joys of self-discovery and personal growth.

RESOURCES

Books:

van der Kolk, B. (2014).
The Body Keeps the Score: Brain, Mind, and Body in the Healing of Trauma.
Viking.

Brown, B. (2012).
Daring Greatly: How the Courage to Be Vulnerable Transforms the Way We Live, Love, Parent, and Lead.
Gotham Books.

Fisher, J. (2017).
Healing the Fragmented Selves of Trauma Survivors: Overcoming Internal Self-Alienation.
Routledge.

Maté, G. (2003).
When the Body Says No: The Cost of Hidden Stress.
Knopf Canada.

Forward, S., & Frazier, D. (1989).
Toxic Parents: Overcoming Their Hurtful Legacy and Reclaiming Your Life.
Bantam.

Articles:

Herman, J. L. (1992).
Complex PTSD: A syndrome in survivors of prolonged and repeated trauma.
Journal of Traumatic Stress, 5(3), 377-391.

Levine, P. A. (1997).
Waking the Tiger: Healing Trauma.
North Atlantic Books.

Smith, M., Robinson, L., & Segal, J (2022).
Dealing with a Toxic Family or Parents: Recognizing, Handling, and Avoiding Unhealthy Relationships.
HelpGuide.org.

Parker, K. (2021).
The Lifelong Effects of Toxic Parenting and How to Break the Cycle.
Psych Central

Websites:

Mindful.
http://www.mindful.org.

Psych Central.
http://www.psychcentral.com.

RAINN.
RAINN.org: Rape, Abuse & Incest National Network.
http://www.rainn.org.

Talkspace.
Talkspace: Online Therapy with Licensed Therapists.
http://www.talkspace.com.

The Mighty.
The Mighty: a digital health community.
http://www.themighty.com.

ABOUT THE AUTHOR

Meet S.Y. Vidal, an artist at heart who thrives on creativity. Whether drawing, painting, writing, or diving into the psychological thrills of a horror movie, Vidal lives for artistic expression. Oh, and let's not forget the cats—each one is a muse and practically part of the writing team.

While Vidal's degree might not be in psychology, it still hangs proudly next to his priceless artwork—both testaments to the school of life. Let's say his wisdom comes less from textbooks and more from a curriculum set by a harsh yet enlightening life journey. It's the advice you'd get from a friend who may not know Pi to the 20th decimal but knows how to piece together a broken soul. Vidal writes how he talks—no holds barred, heartfelt, and relatable. The aim? To dive deep but keep it real, just like a chat with an old friend who's seen it all.

When the pen is down, and the paints are packed away, Vidal immerses himself in the rich landscapes and vibrant culture of Puerto Rico. The island's natural beauty is not just a backdrop but a source of endless inspiration. Ultimately, Vidal stands by the mantra that the only person who can truly save you is yourself. It's a belief that anchors him and acts as the cornerstone of his work. Through his books, art, and voice, he empowers others to dig deep and discover their hidden wellsprings of strength.

YOUR VOICE MATTERS

If this book has been a companion on your healing journey, if it's helped you understand, process, or begin to heal from childhood trauma, I would be deeply grateful if you would take a moment to share your experience.

Your review isn't just words on a page—it's a beacon of hope for others who might be struggling, feeling alone, or searching for understanding. By sharing how this book touched your life, you could be the lifeline someone else needs to take their first step towards healing.

Would you consider leaving a review on:

- Amazon
- Goodreads
- Google Books

Every review, every shared story, has the power to make a difference. Thank you for being brave, for your journey, and for potentially helping another soul find their path to healing.

With gratitude & hope,

ALSO AVAILABLE

rosemary woodlands
publishing

Signed Copies Available @
www.syvidalbooks.com

www.ingramcontent.com/pod-product-compliance
Lightning Source LLC
Chambersburg PA
CBHW010936120626
46554CB00007B/2483